KU-627-489

To Mum,   September 26th, 1983

On your Birthday!
Have a Memorable Day,
                Love,
                        Peter

ABOVE Pale-blue funnel-necked top, £22, and paisley skirt, £25, Topshop Petite range, selected stores nationwide (0800 7318284). Ponyskin mules, £145, Russell & Bromley, 24-25 New Bond Street, London W1 (0171-629 6903)

FAR LEFT Pink cami-top, £35, Diesel, available at Selfridges (0171-255 3007).
Short-leg indigo jeans (from 24in), £55, Diesel, 43 Earlham Street, London WC2 (0171-833 2255). Pink headscarf, £4, Topshop as before. Feather necklace, £12.99, Johnny Loves Rosie mail order (0171-375 3574)

ABOVE LEFT Cowboy hat, £12.95, Naf Naf, 13-15 King's Road, London SW3 (0171-730 7672). Black halter-necked top with yellow beading detail, £27.50, Morgan, selected stores nationwide (0171-499 4101). Black cropped trousers, £24.99, Next Petite, stores nationwide (0845 600 7000). Beaded choker (worn around arm), £3, Topshop as before.
Yellow sandals, £285, Gina Couture, 9 Old Bond Street, London W1 (0171-409 7090)

TOP Mint linen dress with drawstring neckline (from sizes 6-16), £27.50, La Redoute mail order (0500 777 777). Feather necklace (worn around wrist), from a selection, Johnny Loves Rosie, as before

LEFT Pink floral dress (from sizes 6-16), £170, Whistles stores nationwide (0171-487 4484). Cowboy hat, £12.95, Naf Naf, as before. Blue thong high-heeled mules, to order, Gina, 189 Sloane Street, London SW1 (0171-235 2932). Pink tinted sunglasses, £109, Cutler & Gross, 15 Knightsbridge Green, London SW1 (0171-581 2250)

Tetilla, the mild and creamy Galician cheese, is shaped in the form of a nippled breast, which might help to explain the local saying that "cheese tastes like kisses"

'For the gourmet traveller cheese is yet another edible purchase to stuff into the suitcase along with chorizo'

In the best-known book in the Spanish language, Spain gets a pretty poor write-up. The vast, desolate plains of La Mancha are the backdrop for the peregrinations of the hapless Don Quixote and, at one point, in an unfortunate passing reference, Cervantes describes the local Manchego cheese as "harder than if it had been made out of sand and lime".

"That was in 1605 — the good news is that things have improved a lot. Today, the Knight of the Sorrowful Countenance would struggle to recognise the delicious aristocratic cheese which displays his silhouette marching across the label, but the milk still comes from the Manchega breed of sheep. A cheese of many guises, depending on age, it can be soft, crumbly and creamy, or well-matured, hard and dry. The rind is imprinted with the distinct basketweave pattern of the mould, woven from plaited strands of esparto grass.

Spain has hundreds of cheeses, almost as many as castles, ranging from idiosyncratic local farmhouse to bland, mass-produced ones, each fashioned from a distinctive mix of geography, climate and culture. Until relatively recently, says Mariano Sanz Pech of the Consortium of Spanish Traditional Cheeses (look for the "Quesos Tradicionales" label), many Spanish cheeses were virtually unknown beyond their locality.

In 1988, as a result of encroaching industrialisation, a national survey catalogued the nation's artisan cheese.

The result is that Spain has 16 DO (Denominación de Origen) cheeses, many of which are making their mark on international cheese competitions. No longer are the best cheeses kept in Spain and the worst sent abroad. For the gourmet traveller, it is yet another edible purchase to stuff into the suitcase along with the saffron and rice, pimento and chorizo. "The problem is how do you say: "Just 500g of Garrotxa, please"?

Steven Jenkins, author of *The Cheese Primer*, rates Spanish cheese as among the best in the world and several years ago forecast the rise to fame of the Extremaduran cheese, Torta Del Casar. A quick-ripening spring ewes' milk cheese, it is tangy, runny and round, the rind acting as a container with the paste soft enough to be scooped out with a spoon. The Spanish describe it as a *senor queso*, a serious cheese.

Jenkins's views are echoed by Katherine Caplin of importers Brindisa: "People are waking up to Spanish cheese."

Carole Faulkner, of the Cheese Shop in Chester, who stocks a wide range of artisan Spanish cheeses, agrees: "Many of my customers go to Spain on holiday and have really got into the local cheese. People are also doing special dinner parties — and Spanish

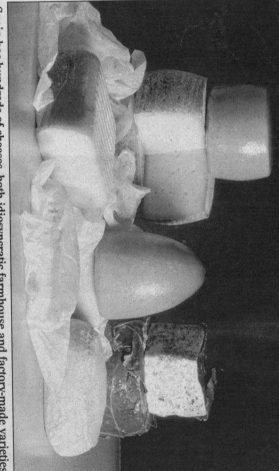

Spain has hundreds of cheeses, both idiosyncratic farmhouse and factory-made varieties

themes are proving extremely popular."

Damp and green, the lush north-west regions of Spain are the home of many fine cheeses. The first in Spain to be awarded DO status was Roncal, an intensely flavoured ewes' milk cheese from Navarra. Other cows' milk cheeses are the buttery Cantabria, and Tetilla, the mild and creamy Galician cheese, named and shaped in the form of a nippled breast — which might

help to explain the local saying, quoted by food writer Maria Jose Sevilla, that "cheese tastes like kisses".

Unusually for a Mediterranean cheese, the Minorcan Mahon is made from the milk of Friesian cows, originally brought to the island by the British in the 18th century. Slightly salty, with a spicy aroma, its cushion shape derives from the practice of moulding the cheese in a knotted cloth, and the orangey colour from

rubbing the rind with butter and olive oil mixed with paprika to protect it from the flies.

Among the many goats' cheeses, Montenebro, a soft, ash-coated log from Avila, sells out at The Bluebird restaurant in London soon after it comes in. Garrotxa, a pleasantly sharp version of a traditional Catalonian goats' cheese, was developed by a new generation of "neo-rural" cheesemakers who left their professional city lives for the good life.

Spanish ewes'-milk cheeses are also particularly fine: full-flavoured and firm-textured Zamorano is made with milk from Churra sheep, and La Serena, a rare and exquisite cheese from Extremadura, is

made, unusually, with milk from Merino sheep and natural rennet from cardoons.

Another historic cheese, Idiazabal, a seasonal ewes' milk cheese from the Basque country, is much sought after and prize-winning artisan specimens have been known to fetch up to $1,000 (£640) a kilo at local fairs.

The Spanish seldom cook with cheese, apart from a recipe for Manchego fried in olive oil and various salsas de Cabrales. Mostly, it is served as tapas or with bread and wine, or after dinner with sweetmeats made from dried fruit, nuts and muscatel wine, or with membrillo (quince cheese). This latter combination has proved so popular with her customers that Anne-Marie Dawson of the Fine Cheese Company in Bath and Cheltenham now offers it, with a fine Manchego, as a mail order gift pack (£17.95 inc p&p; 01225 483407).

Increasingly, chefs are looking for other ways in which to plunder this treasure-trove of cheeses. Mató, creamy, fresh goats' cheese, has long been popular in Catalonia as a dessert drizzled with honey.

Peter Gordon, of the Sugar Club in London, pairs Garrotxa with rocket and organic oyster mushrooms deep-fried in paprika-flavoured batter.

Spanish cheese has been a secret for too long. If, as has oft been quoted, cheese is milk's leap towards immortality, the Spanish varieties deserve their place with the gods.

MICHAEL POWELL

TIMES 24 JULY 1999

The Cheese Book

The CHEESE Book

Richard Widcombe

OMEGA BOOKS

ACKNOWLEDGEMENTS

The following organisations and companies provided information and assistance in the compilation of this book: the Australian Dairy Corporation; the Danish Cheese Export Board; the English Country Cheese Council; Norwegian Dairies; the Dutch Dairy Bureau; the German Dairy Board; Alta Lipids Australia Pty Ltd; the photograph of Brick cheese was supplied by the American Dairy Association; the photograph of Liederkranz cheese was provided by Borden Foods, Ohio; the illustrations of stages in the cheesemaking process were provided by the Australian Dairy Board. Works consulted during the research were Androuet's *Guide du Fromage*, Marquis and Haskell's *The Cheese Book*, the US Department of Agriculture's publication *Cheeses of the World* and Simon's *Cheeses of the World*.

Special thanks to Mr David Golante of The Cheese Board, Manhattan, New York, for his advice on American cheeses and also to Maureen and Ian Nathan of the International Cheese Shop, Crows Nest, Sydney, for general consultation on the book.

This edition published 1983 by Omega Books Ltd,
1 West Street, Ware, Hertfordshire, under licence
from the proprietor.

Copyright © Daniel O'Keefe Publications 1978

All rights reserved. No part of this publication
may be reproduced, stored in a retrieval system,
or transmitted, in any form or by any means, electronic,
mechanical, photocopying, recording or otherwise,
without the prior permission of the publishers.

ISBN 0 907853 06 4

Printed and bound in Hong Kong by South China Printing Co.

CONTENTS

THE WORLD OF CHEESE   7

THE HISTORY OF CHEESE	8
CHEESEMAKING	8
CHEESE TYPES	12
KEEPING AND STORING	16
CHEESE AND WINE	16
RINDLESS AND CANNED CHEESES	16
CHEESE LANGUAGE	17

CHEESES A TO Z   21

INDEX   158

THE WORLD OF CHEESE

Cheese is one of the most varied and subtle foods in the world. In taste cheese can be bland, buttery, innocuous, rich, creamy, pungent, sharp, salty or lightly delicate. In texture it can be hard enough to chip off in flakes, so soft and runny that it needs to be eaten with a spoon—or at any one of a dozen points of softness and firmness between these two extremes. In aroma, cheese can be rank and overpowering enough to turn the stomach of the strongest man (and still be eaten with relish by devotees), delicately aromatic or virtually unnoticeable. Cheese can serve as the perfect companion for wines, a superbly satisfying finale to a gourmet meal or simply as a basic nourishing foodstuff for family snacks.

It is this variety of character that has made cheese so appreciated as a food for hundreds, even thousands, of years. The reason for this is that the cheesemaking process, while following the same broad pattern, is subjected to numerous variations in types of milk, cheesemaking techniques and the length of the time given to maturing. The differences in textures, flavours and aromas of different cheeses are the result of these numerous variations.

Thus cheeses offer an enormous range—from the rich delicacy of a Brie or a Camembert to the full 'bite' of a mature Cheddar and the sharp piercing saltiness of a Feta. And while every cheese is not to every taste, it is fair to say that almost everyone can find a cheese to suit his or her taste.

Cheese is also one of the most nutritious of foods. A cheese with a fat content of 48 per cent has a protein content in the region of 23-25 per cent, making the protein value of 210 g (7 oz) of such a cheese equal to 300 g (10 oz) of meat. In one solid, compact form, cheese also contains calcium, phosphorus, mineral salts and varying amounts of A and B and other vitamins.

Of course most cheeses are also high in calories, a fact that causes many people concerned with their weight to be wary.

A cheese's calorie count can be judged from the fat content which most cheeses have detailed on their packaging. The fat content refers to the percentage of butterfat in the dry matter of the cheese. The Dutch, for example, class their cheeses as:

- full-cream cheese—48 per cent fat content
- 40+ —at least 40 per cent fat content
- 20+ —at least 20 per cent fat content
- 4+ (skim milk cheese)—4 per cent fat content

While it is true that many cheeses do have a high calorie count, this does not apply to them all. Cottage Cheese, depending on whether it is creamed or not, has a butterfat content varying between 4 and 15 per cent; the German sour curd cheeses such as Harz and Mainz have a fat content under 10 per cent, and Australia has recently developed a fat modified Cheddar-style cheese marketed as Altapol.

It is worth remembering, too, the overall composition of cheese when considering its fat content. The softer the cheese the higher its moisture content will be. Thus soft cheeses such as Camembert and Brie can contain up to 50 per cent water—therefore their fat content (45-50 per cent) need only be counted against half of what you eat. On the other hand, the fat content of Emmentaler (45 per cent) cannot be considered so reducible as Emmentaler is a hard cheese which has had a large degree of moisture drained from it.

At the top end of the fat-content scale lie the double and triple crème cheeses, which can have a fat content of from 60 to 75 per cent. If you develop a passion for these, it is probably best that you take up jogging.

THE HISTORY OF CHEESE

Most authorities consider that cheese was first made in the Middle East. The earliest type was a form of sour milk which came into being when it was discovered that domesticated animals could be milked. A legendary story has it that cheese was 'discovered' by an unknown Arab nomad. He is said to have filled a saddlebag with milk to sustain him on a journey across the desert by horse. After several hours riding he stopped to quench his thirst, only to find that the milk had separated into a pale watery liquid and solid white lumps. Because the saddlebag, which was made from the stomach of a young animal, contained a coagulating enzyme known as rennin, the milk had been effectively separated into curds and whey by the combination of the rennin, the hot sun and the galloping motions of the horse. The nomad, unconcerned with technical details, found the whey drinkable and the curds edible.

Cheese was known to the ancient Sumerians four thousand years before the birth of Christ. The ancient Greeks credited Aristaeus, a son of Apollo and Cyrene, with its discovery; it is mentioned in the Old Testament.

In the Roman era cheese really came into its own. Cheesemaking was done with skill and knowledge and reached a high standard. By this time the ripening process had been developed and it was known that various treatments and conditions under storage resulted in different flavours and characteristics.

The larger Roman houses had a separate cheese kitchen, the *caseale*, and also special areas where cheese could be matured. In large towns home-made cheese could be taken to a special centre to be smoked. Cheese was served on the tables of the nobility and travelled to the far corners of the Roman Empire as a regular part of the rations of the legions.

During the Middle Ages, monks became innovators and developers and it is to them we owe many of the classic varieties of cheese marketed today. During the Renaissance period cheese suffered a drop in popularity, being considered unhealthy, but it regained favour by the nineteenth century, the period that saw the start of the move from farm to factory production.

Cutting the cheese curd before 'cheddaring'.

CHEESEMAKING

Cheese is made from milk; in the main it is made from cow's milk but there are many varieties made from sheep's milk and goat's milk. Cheese is also made from the milk of buffaloes (Mozzarella is one), reindeer, asses, camels and most domesticated herbivores (let it be added, however, that it is unlikely that your local cheese supplier is going to be pressing huge stocks of reindeer's, asses' or camel's milk cheese upon you).

The basic principle involved in making all natural cheese is to coagulate or curdle the milk so that it forms into curds (milky white lumps) and whey (a thin liquid). As anyone knows who has left milk unrefrigerated for a period, milk will curdle quite naturally. The milk sours and forms into an acid curd. This is the basis of nearly all cheesemaking (whey cheeses are the exception, being made from the whey of the milk rather than the curds). Today's methods help the curdling process by the addition of a *starter* (a bacterial culture which produces lactic acid) and *rennet* (a

The beginning of the 'cheddaring' process. The drained cheese curd is turned and stacked at the bottom of the cheese vat at intervals of ten to fifteen minutes for about one-and-a-half hours.

Salting—here the cheese is being immersed in a brine bath. Salting plays an important role in rind formation.

Milling Cheddar cheese. The cheese is milled into small curd pieces, salted, then placed in cloth-lined metal hoops.

Storing and maturing blue vein cheese. Note the inoculation needles in the foreground. These needles allow air to penetrate into the body of the cheese to promote the growth of the veining.

substance obtained from the stomach linings of young calves which contains a coagulating enzyme which speeds the separation of liquids and solids).

The least sophisticated cheeses are the fresh, unripened varieties typified by Cottage Cheese. These are made by warming the milk and letting it stand, treating it with a lactic starter to help the acid development and then cutting and draining the whey from the cheese. The cheese is then packed and marketed without further ripening. This is the simplest, most basic form of cheese.

Cheeses that undergo a ripening process (also known as a curing, maturing or ageing process) are all treated with rennet. Before the ripening process begins, they go through a sequence of operations which, while following the same general pattern, varies from cheese to cheese. Basically, this sequence is:

- milk is warmed
- a starter culture and rennet are added
- the milk coagulates into a single huge curd
- the curd is stirred and cut to drain off whey
- the curd is heated, sometimes pressed, to remove more whey
- the curd is moulded and shaped into a cheese, salting taking place before or after this process
- the cheese is matured under controlled conditions.

Variations on the cheesemaking process start with the milk. It may be taken from a morning or an evening milking, or from a combination of both. Before the milk is set a colouring agent may be added to it, the most widely used one being annatto, a vegetable dye taken from a South American plant. This produces an amber-orange-yellow colour. The milk may be skimmed of its cream content or have cream added to it. The quality of the milk, its richness, its acid content, the degree to which it is heated, even the breed of cow that is used, the grass she feeds on, the soil and the climate—all these factors influence the final cheese.

So does the amount of rennet used, the way the cheese is pressed, the heating of the curds, the degree of salting, the number of times the cheese is turned from one side to another while it is maturing, how the cheese is brushed, scraped or washed and the ingredients used to treat the cheese (Appenzell is immersed for a period in a mixture of white wine and spices, Maroilles is bathed with beer, Feta matures in brine and so forth.)

During the ripening period, the two most important factors are the length of the maturing time (it can vary from two weeks to seven years) and the temperature at which the cheese is matured.

It is during this time that the micro-organisms play their part. They may be present naturally in the milk or in the atmosphere of the curing room, or they can be artificially introduced.

Blue veined cheeses are inoculated with a *Penicillium* spore which creates their aroma, flavour and bluish or greenish veining. Such cheeses are internally moulded and ripen from the inside out. On the other hand, cheeses such as Camembert and Brie have their surfaces treated with a different type of *Penicillium* spore which creates a downy white mould (known as a bloomy or flowery rind): this makes them surface ripened cheeses.

Many surface ripened cheeses have their surfaces smeared with a bacterial broth. With others the bacteria is in the atmosphere of the curing chambers. These cheeses are called washed rind varieties as they must be washed regularly during their ripening period (longer than for Camembert or Brie) to prevent their interiors drying out. The washings also help promote an even bacterial growth across the surfaces of the cheeses. As this washing can be done with liquids as diverse as salt water and brandy, it also plays a part in the final flavour of the cheese.

The rinds of the cheeses are formed during the ripening process, many quite naturally. Some, as we have seen, artificially. Rinds may be brushed, washed, oiled, treated with a covering of paraffin wax or simply not touched at all. Traditional Cheddars are wrapped around with a cotton bandage. The rind's basic function is to protect the interior of the cheese and allow it to ripen harmoniously. Its presence thus affects the final flavour of the cheese. Salting plays an important role in rind formation. Heavily salted cheeses develop a thick, tough outer rind, typified by the Swiss range of cheeses. Cheddar, another natural-rind cheese, is less salted than the Swiss varieties, and consequently has a much thinner rind.

A batch of Australian Gouda cheese maturing.

Mention too needs to be made of pasteurisation. On the Continent, many cheeses are made from raw, unpasteurised milk. Outside Europe, however, most cheeses are made from pasteurised milk. American federal laws, for example state that all unripened cheese must be made from pasteurised milk and so also must all ripened cheeses, unless they are aged for a period of at least sixty days. Similarly, all English and Australian cheese is made from pasteurised milk. While the interests of hygiene may be best served in this way, cheeses made from pasteurised milk never develop the full character and personality of cheeses made from unpasteurised milk, simply because many of the micro-organisms responsible have been effectively destroyed.

Processed cheese, as opposed to natural cheese, takes this one stage further. Here the actual cheese (usually a combination of two cheeses), rather than the milk, is subjected to a heat treatment at a given point. Because of this the cheese does not continue to mature and develop in flavour, but remains constant in taste throughout its life.

CHEESE TYPES

Cheese can be placed into various family groups or types. The groupings are, however, somewhat arbitrary and vary from authority to authority. The Australian Dairy Board, for example, classes all cheeses made in Australia as fresh, soft, firm or hard. The Board classes as fresh cheeses Cottage, Cream, and Ricotta; as firm cheeses Cheddar, Cheshire, Edam, Gouda, Provolone, Taffel, Samsoe and Swiss (Emmentaler); and as hard cheeses Parmesan, Pecorino, Pepato and Romano.

The US Department of Agriculture classes cheeses as very hard, hard, semi-soft or soft. It considers Cheddar a hard cheese rather than firm and blue veins as semi-soft rather than soft. The Department, in a publication first produced in 1953, also states that there are about eighteen types of natural cheeses, listing them as Brick, Camembert, Cheddar, Cottage, Cream, Edam, Gouda, Hand, Limburger, Neufchâtel, Parmesan, Provolone, Romano, Roquefort, Sapsago, Swiss, Trappist and whey

cheese. The Department adds, however, that such a grouping, while informative, is 'imperfect and incomplete'.

The French cheese expert Pierre Androuet, in his book *Guide de Fromage*, an excellent and detailed study principally of French cheeses, is more exact. Apart from fresh cheeses and processed cheeses he classifies cheeses into six family groups by their nature and type of rind. They are: bloomy-rind cheeses such as Camembert and Brie; wash-rind cheeses such as Limburger, Maroilles and Livarot; natural-rind goat's milk cheeses; blue veins; semi-soft uncooked pressed cheeses such as Saint Paulin; and hard or cooked cheeses such as Parmesan and Emmentaler.

For the layman, probably the easiest way to identify cheese types is to place the cheese in groupings based on how they are made and similarities of appearance and flavour. The classification used in this book attempts this. It should be said that although not all cheeses within a grouping will taste alike, they should be more similar in taste than cheeses placed in other groups. It will also be seen that some cheeses can be placed in more than one group.

Fresh, unripened cheeses: These are cheeses which do not undergo a maturing process and include Cottage, Cream and Ricotta. In taste they are the mildest, least flavoursome of all cheeses. They are usually not salted.

Double and Triple crèmes: These cheeses have been heavily enriched with cream during their manufacturing process. The double crèmes have a fat content of 60 per cent, and the triple crèmes a 75 per cent fat content. This makes them all exceptionally rich, creamy and luscious. Some of them do not undergo a ripening process, so they can also be classed as unripened cheeses. Petit Suisse is a case in point. Although it is not ripened, its fat content can vary between 60 and 75 per cent. Other double and triple crèmes are cured for about three weeks before marketing and develop a very thin, downy rind. These include Boursault, Brillat-Savarin and Excelsior. Others such as Blue Castello and Bavarian Blue have a blue veining. While double and triple crèmes can vary in flavour and style, they have in common a degree of richness and creaminess not present in other cheeses.

Bland and buttery: Into this category can be placed a great variety of essentially mild tasting, stable, all-purpose table cheeses. These cheeses are unpronounced in flavour and aroma—which is not to say that they are without distinction. The range is considerable and includes the Samsoe group, Edam, Gouda, Bel Paese and Fontina. Such cheeses are usually firm and supple-textured, easily sliceable and make excellent lunch, breakfast or sandwich snacks. Many are of sufficient quality to be served at end of meals.

Swiss-style cheeses: The most famous of these is Emmentaler with its tough outer rind, distinctive holes or 'eyes' and characteristic mild, sweetish, nutty flavour. Relatives of Emmentaler include Appenzell, Gruyère, Royalp, Sbrinz and Raclette. Swiss-style cheeses usually have tough hard rinds and interiors dotted with holes. These holes are caused by expansion of gas within the cheese curd during the ripening period.

Cheddar-style cheeses: Cheddar is one of the most popular and widely copied cheeses in the world. Cheeses that are 'cheddared' undergo a step in the making process which involves them being cut into pieces and stacked and turned at the bottom of the cheese vat for a period. The archetypal Cheddar cheese is firm-textured, yellow in colour with a clean, mellow taste which develops a sharp and tangy bite the further it matures. English cheeses such as Gloucester, Cheshire, Leicester, Lancashire, Derby, Wensleydale and Caerphilly all belong to the Cheddar family. Even Stilton, a blue vein, is Cheddar based. America, Australia, Canada and New Zealand all make varieties of Cheddar in varying degrees of strength. Vermont is one of the best-known American types and the Canadian Cheddars, made from unpasteurised milk, are highly rated. Cantal is a French Cheddar-style cheese and Kashkaval is a distant Greek relative made from sheep's milk.

Extra-hard cheeses: The majority of these cheeses are the Italian Grana style. They have an exceptionally hard, brittle texture which makes them suitable for grating and are known for their exquisitely sharp, piquant flavour.

Cheeses of this type can be matured for up to three years. Parmesan is the best known of the group but the Swiss Sbrinz and Sapsago cheeses also fit into the category. Saanen, also Swiss, is sometimes matured for seven years. Young versions of some grating cheeses are used as table cheeses.

Monastery cheeses: Cheeses in this group are often linked historically in that they have monastic origins. Such cheeses as Port Salut, Saint Paulin, the various forms of Trappist cheese made throughout the world, Esrom and Harvarti have similarities of taste, although varying degrees of strength of flavour and aroma. Several mountain cheeses, such as Beaumont and Reblochon, are also classified as monastery type cheeses. The majority of monastery cheeses are of the washed rind variety.

Blue veins: These cheeses are characterised by their internal veining of blue, blue-black or green, and their pungent aromas and tangy flavours. All blue-vein cheeses are internally ripened after being inoculated with a *Penicillium* spore. They are usually classed as soft cheeses but can be crumbly in texture. Some, however, are exceptionally soft, even to the point of spreadability. Roquefort, Stilton and Gorgonzola are considered the three best blue veins in the world.

Camembert and Brie types: These cheeses are known as bloomy or flowery-rind cheeses because of the light, downy white rind that grows on their surfaces, the result of their being treated with the *Penicillium candidum* spore. The interior paste of this sort of cheese is soft and straw yellow in colour. If the cheese is at its peak, the paste bulges out from beneath the rind when the cheese is cut. Tangy, richly delicate and delicious in flavour, Camembert and Brie are widely copied, but the French versions, of which there are many, are generally acknowledged as the best and the most full-flavoured. Other cheeses of this type include Carré de l'Est, Coulommiers and Chaource.

Goat's milk cheeses: Distinctively different in taste to cow's milk cheeses, these cheeses come in a variety of shapes and sizes such as pyramids, cones and cylinders, all usually quite

13

small. All have a characteristic barnyard or 'goaty' quality to their flavour, but whether this is mild or pronounced depends on how long the cheese has been aged. Some are quite delicate; others are ferociously pungent and rank. All French goat's milk cheeses are called *chèvres*—and today many are made from a mixture of goat's milk and cow's or sheep's milk.

Sheep's milk cheeses: Like goat's milk cheeses, these cheeses taste quite different to cow's milk varieties. Their flavour ranges from mild to sharp. Some are noticeably salty, the result of being matured in brine. Many of the traditional Greek cheeses fall into this category, Feta being best known. Others, like Kashkaval and Kasseri, have a noticeable 'sheepy' flavour —a sourish tang, distinctive and attractive and, like many goat's milk cheeses, vaguely 'barnyardy'.

Spiced or flavoured cheeses: Many cheeses have their flavours enhanced by the addition of a variety of herbs and spices. Derby Sage has a greenish hue due to sage being introduced to the cheese curd during the making process (Vermont Sage is the American equivalent); Leyden is treated with caraway and cumin seeds; and Boursin, a triple-crème cheese, is marketed in flavoured versions ranging from pepper to garlic. Other cheeses may be studded with walnuts, covered with grape seeds or treated with cloves. The English are now producing several of their traditional lines flavoured with beer, wine, cider, port and chives.

Smoked cheeses: Smoked cheese is simply a cheese variety, often Cheddar or Emmentaler, which has been treated and flavoured with smoke. Most of this type of cheese is processed. It is often made in traditional sausage shapes. In most cases the smoke flavour is produced by chemicals rather than by hanging the cheeses over a fire. Smoked cheeses are often additionally flavoured with ingredients ranging from caraway seeds to a textured vegetable protein tasting like ham.

Whey cheeses: While the great majority of cheeses are made from the curds of the milk, there are some which are made from the whey. Gjetöst, a cheese totally distinctive in looks and taste, is one. It has milk sugar (lactose) and cream added to it during the making process and looks like a chunk of chocolate fudge. Ricotta, already classed as an unripened cheese, is also made from whey but is basically an Italian version of Cottage Cheese. It has nothing in common, in either taste or appearance, with Gjetöst—except that it is a whey cheese.

Strong-smelling cheeses: Probably the best known cheese in this category is Limburger, Belgian in origin but often thought of as German due to its great popularity in that country. Cheeses that possess a truly powerful aroma are usually of the washed rind variety. For many people the aroma is both the beginning and the end of the acquaintance. A legendary story about Limburger recounts the uproar that was created in a small town in Green County, Wisconsin, when a cartload of ripened Limburgers was left unattended in a main street. The fact is that cheeses such as Limburger, Maroilles and Livarot are extremely pungent smelling, not to say rank, and overpowering. In Limburger's case, its bark is somewhat less than its bite, for the cheese's taste is not as strong as its smell. Maroilles and Livarot, however, are both strong-smelling and strong-tasting, as are the German matured varieties of sour curd cheeses such as Harz and Mainz (the American version of this style of cheese is known as Hand). Brick and Liederkranz, the two cheeses that are considered genuine American originals, are also noted for their distinctive aromas, but unless well aged they are not overpronounced in taste.

Processed cheese: All processed cheese has its ripening process arrested at a given point by heat treatment. It is usually made from one or two cheese types blended together and can never develop the individuality of flavour of natural cheese because the micro-organisms that create such things are effectively killed off. For many people processed cheeses taste 'plastic' and innocuous but nevertheless they are enormously popular—partly because of their keeping properties, their economy and their blandness. Today there is an enormous range of processed cheese on the market, flavoured by a staggering variety of ingredients which range from salmon to pineapple.

A selection of Provolone and Mozzarella cheeses (photo by Russell Cockayne)

KEEPING AND STORING

It was tempting to discuss the maximum time that a cheese will keep, but as most people will buy cheese by the piece, there seemed little point in doing this. Once a cheese has been cut it loses the protection of its rind and starts to deteriorate.

If you buy a whole cheese and store it correctly it is quite possible it will keep for more than a year, if not cut. Storing whole, uncut cheeses, however, is an involved business. Besides needing the right conditions—a cool, moist, well ventilated room, free of draughts—cheeses need a certain amount of attention. Remember too, that cheese, like wine, is a living substance that will continue to develop the longer it is stored, and you may end up with a cheese whose flavour is quite different from the one you originally envisaged.

The amount of time any cheese will keep is dependent on its moisture content. Fresh cheeses with a high moisture content need to be eaten within a short time after purchase, while extra-hard grating cheese will keep almost indefinitely. Correctly stored, a firm-textured cheese like Cheddar, when cut, will keep for several weeks, as will a semi-soft cheese like Saint Paulin. Bloomy rind cheese such as Brie and Camembert have a limited life when cut and should be eaten as soon as possible.

Probably the best course for the average cheese buyer is to buy in small quantities—that is, buy only what you are capable of eating within one to two weeks. A major exception are the hard grating cheeses such as Parmesan. A cut piece of Parmesan cheese, provided it is well wrapped and stored, will keep for a considerable length of time.

Cut cheese should be kept in a refrigerator, wrapped in airtight aluminium foil, plastic film or bags. If you are storing several types of cheese, they should of course be wrapped individually. Before serving, the cheese should be removed from the refrigerator for at least two hours so that it is given sufficient time to reach room temperature before consumption, otherwise you will not get the benefit of its true flavour. Cheese for immediate consumption can be kept under a cheese dome. It is a useful trick to place under the edge of the dome a small object such as a piece of sugar to allow the water vapour given off by the cheese to escape. Do not store cheese under a dome. Cheese can be frozen, but this is not really recommended. Texture and flavour are likely to be affected—and for the worse.

Should a mould spot develop on a cheese, simply cut it off. The rest of the cheese will not be adversely affected, unless the mould is widespread.

CHEESE AND WINE

Cheese and wine are a natural combination but they will not join forces indiscriminately. A cheese with a full aroma and strong flavour will not go well with a delicate wine that has a subtle bouquet—the cheese will overwhelm the wine. A practical rule of thumb is—the more body the wine has, the more full-flavoured the cheese may be. So do not serve a soft-flavoured little-accented cheese with a heavy wine. Similarly, do not serve a light and elegant wine with a sharp and tangy cheese.

In this book only the general characteristics of the wine style most suited to the particular cheese are described. Although there is a world trend towards describing wines by the grape variety from which they are made and the regional characteristics of the area in which the grapes are grown, this trend is not yet universally established. The wines in this book have consequently been described in general terms as sweet or dry, red or white, fruity, full-bodied, aged, et cetera.

RINDLESS AND CANNED CHEESES

The function of a cheese's rind is to protect the interior of the cheese so that it can ripen and develop harmoniously. A well closed, firm, natural rind keeps the cheese in shape and makes it practically impossible for anything undesirable from outside to penetrate. On bloomy and washed rind cheeses the degree of bacterial activity which takes place on and in the rind affects the final flavour of the interior of the cheese.

Rindless cheeses are basically a packaging and marketing asset for the manufacturer. What happens is that after a cheese is formed and salted, it is sealed in a plastic wrapping or film in which the cheese ripens and in which it is often marketed. No rind forms on the cheese, the plastic doing the job of protecting the cheese.

The savings to the manufacturer on this type of cheese are obvious; from the consumer's viewpoint the cheese will keep longer when kept in its plastic wrapper and there is no wastage of cheese (no rind to cut away). But as there is no rind there is a loss in flavour. Rindless cheeses are milder and blander tasting; they lack depth, individuality and intensity of flavour because the rind which helps create such things does not exist.

Should rinds be eaten with a cheese or cut away? Certain cheeses have hard, tough rinds which are obviously not designed to be eaten and will have to be removed. But with cheeses like Brie and Camembert and numerous other bloomy and washed rind types this is not the case. Indeed, many people find the rind on a Camembert or Brie 'the best part'.

Nevertheless, there are several lofty authorities on the subject who insist that the rind should be removed from any cheese, regardless of type, to appreciate the true flavour. The man or woman who does this with every cheese encountered can be considered either a true connoisseur or someone with the fastidious eating habits of a sixteenth century Spanish grandee.

Canned Camemberts and Bries are a fairly popular feature of the cheese market today. Of these it should be said that their major advantage is that they can be stored almost indefinitely, but in taste they are a long way from fresh Camembert or Brie. Any food that is packaged in cans has to be subjected to heat treatment to prevent it deteriorating. In effect, a canned cheese has been pasteurised (not just the milk from which the cheese has been made, but the cheese itself). Such a cheese can never have the quality, subtlety and depth of flavour of a natural cheese. At best a useful standby and relatively economical compared to the price of fresh Brie or Camembert—but not to be compared to the two great classic cheeses of France.

A word too about the composition of this book. Cheeses are listed in alphabetical order. Those that the average cheese buyer is likely to come across are described in considerable detail, as are others that are unusual or interesting. Besides a description of the cheese, its fat content is given, wines which will complement it are suggested, along with serving tips. The type or group to which the cheese belongs is also detailed and each cheese's aroma is broadly defined as 'pronounced' or 'unpronounced'. When a cheese has an interesting background or story associated with it, this is mentioned. Related cheeses are described more briefly to avoid repetition, and cross-referenced to the cheese to which they are similar.

Dimensions and shapes of individual cheeses and individual brands vary so widely that the dimensions given throughout the book are intended only as a reference to the general size and shape.

Finally, it should be stressed that a cheese purchased outside its country of origin will often taste stronger than one purchased within its country of origin. This is because the cheese will have spent time travelling and in storage. It will have continued to age and develop and thus have gained in strength of flavour.

CHEESE LANGUAGE

Like wine, there is a variety of expressions used in regard to cheese which can cause confusion. The language of the world of cheese can be surrounded by as much mystique, nonsense and pretension as that of wine. This shouldn't be so, of course, and the descriptive terms in this book have been kept as basic as possible.

The following glossary defines expressions used in the book with which some readers might not be familiar and others that might be encountered outside of its pages.

Acid, acidulous: a term used to describe a cheese with a lightly sourish flavour.

Ammoniated, ammoniacal: when certain cheeses are past their prime and overripe they will smell and often taste of ammonia. This particularly applies to soft cheeses such as Brie and Camembert. For those unfamiliar with this smell, it can possibly best be described by imagining a cheese that has been sprayed by a particularly virulent tom cat—a thing to be avoided at all costs!

Annatto: a colouring agent used to colour a great variety of cheeses ranging from English Cheddar to the French Maroilles. Annatto is a dye obtained from a South American plant.

Aroma: a cheese's smell or odour which can vary from lightly aromatic to ferociously overpowering. Note that while most strong smelling cheese will also be strong tasting, this does not apply to all. Limburger is a case in point. The American cheeses Brick and Liederkranz both have distinctive aromas but are not overly strong tasting cheeses unless well aged.

Barnyardy: a descriptive term often used to describe a cheese's aroma and sometimes its taste as well. Many people find goat's milk cheeses barnyardy, particularly aged ones.

Bleu: French name for blue veined cheeses.

Bloomy rind: cheeses that develop a light white down on their surfaces are known as bloomy or flowery rind cheeses. Such a rind develops as a result of the cheese's surface being sprayed with the *Penicillium candidum* spore. The best known cheeses of this type are Camembert and Brie.

Brushed: certain types of natural rind cheeses, cooked and uncooked varieties, have their rinds brushed during the period they spend ripening. This brushing, done by hand or machine, helps the interior of the cheese to keep moist during the ripening period; it also has an effect on the final flavour of the cheese.

Casein: the element of milk which solidifies when coagulation takes place.

Cellar: the room, usually underground, where cheeses are left to ripen. Some cheeses, Roquefort is the most famous, are ripened in caves.

Cheddaring: a cheese that is 'cheddared' has its curd cut into blocks which are turned and stacked at the bottom of the cheese vat at intervals of ten to fifteen minutes for about one-and-a-half hours.

Close: used to describe a cheese's texture. A close textured cheese is one which is smooth, unblemished and devoid of holes or cracks.

Cooked: a step in the cheesemaking process when the cheese curd is heated, sometimes in the surplus whey. Cooked cheeses are all hard cheeses such as Emmentaler and other Swiss types.

Cream: the fatty element of milk.

Creamy: used to describe both the taste and sometimes the texture of certain cheeses.

Curdling: an early stage in cheesemaking when milk coagulates due to the introduction of rennet.

Curing: also known as maturing or ageing— the stage in the cheesemaking process when a cheese is left to ripen.

Crumbly: the condition of a cheese that breaks away when cut—often applicable to blue veins.

Dry matter: the part of the cheese that remains after all moisture is removed. Soft cheeses, such as Brie and Camembert, will, on average, contain about 50 per cent dry matter and 50 per cent water.

Earthy: a descriptive term often used to describe the nature of monastery cheeses.

Fat content: the fat content of cheese refers to the fat content in the dry matter of the cheese. It is usually indicated on the cheese's packaging. The average is 45 per cent but it can be as low as 4 per cent and as high as 75 per cent.

Formaggio: Italian for cheese.

Fresh cheese: a cheese that does not undergo a ripening period—e.g. Cottage Cheese, Cream Cheese, Ricotta.

Fromage: French for cheese.

Gruyère: not only the name of one of the best known Swiss cheeses in the world but also a general name for large cheeses made in France —e.g. Gruyère de Comte, Beaufort, Emmentaler.

Hard: descriptive term for cooked cheeses.

Holes: also called 'eyes', basically openings in the body of cheeses such as Emmentaler, Gruyère and other Swiss types. Such holes are spherical, equally spaced and about the size of cherry stones. The holes are caused by bacterial activity which generates prioponic acid causing gas to expand within the curd.

Kaas: Dutch for cheese.

Käse: German for cheese.

Lactic: milk aroma, sometimes flavour, of certain cheeses.

Micro-organisms: yeasts and ferments present in milk and milk curd.

Monastery: certain cheeses are linked historically in that they were originally developed by monks. They are known as monastery cheeses although they range in flavour and aroma considerably.

Moulds: moulds can be on the surface of cheese or be developed internally. Surface moulds are the result of cheese being treated with the *Penicillium candidum* spore; internal moulds are created by the introduction of *Penicillium glaucum* or *Penicillium roqueforti* spores both to create blue veined cheeses. Certain French goat milk cheeses develop a natural bluish surface mould and some of the newer double crème cheeses have both a surface mould and an internal mould—e.g. Blue Castello, Bavarian Blue, Duet.

Mushroomy: flavour and aroma description of certain soft and semi-soft cheeses, particularly members of the Brie/Camembert family.

Nutty: flavour description of certain cheeses, often refers to a hazelnut flavour.

Open: texture description referring to a cheese which contains openings and holes in its body. The opposite of *close*.

Paraffined: many cheeses are coated with a paraffin wax, particularly those destined for export markets. Edam is probably the best known. The wax protects the cheese.

Pasteurisation: the treatment given to partially sterilised milk.

Paste: the interior of a cheese.

Pronounced: descriptive term for a cheese's aroma or flavour.

Penicillium: moulds that are developed on the surface of bloomy rind cheeses (Camembert, Brie) and internally in blue veins (see *moulds*).

Persille: a French term for a blue vein cheese used in reference to Roquefort because it is the only bleu from sheep's milk.

Piquant: descriptive term for a sharp tasting cheese.

Rennet: a substance obtained from the stomach linings of young calves which contains a coagulating enzyme.

Rind: the protective external surface of a cheese. Rinds can be natural or artificially created, thick or thin, hard or soft, washed, oiled, brushed or paraffined. Their prime role is to protect the cheese's interior and allow it to ripen and develop harmoniously. Their presence affects the final flavour of the interior of the cheese.

Skimmed milk: when part or all of the cream has been removed from milk, the milk is referred to as skimmed. Cheeses made from such milk generally have a lower fat content than average; some (but not all) are quite pronounced in taste.

Starter: a bacterial culture which produces lactic acid.

Supple: descriptive term used to describe a cheese's texture—firm but not hard, pliable and resilient.

Tangy: descriptive term used to denote a cheese's flavour usually meaning sharp, distinctive, flavoursome.

Texture: a cheese's texture can be soft, firm, hard, semi-soft, supple, waxy, open, close and so on. Texture is largely dependent on its moisture content—the softer the cheese the higher its moisture content.

Washed rind cheeses: the rinds of certain cheeses are regularly washed while they are being ripened. The purpose of this is to keep the cheese moist, supple and to ensure it does not dry out. Such washings can be done with elements as varied as salt water or brandy—thus the washing plays a part in the cheese's final flavour. Some of the strongest smelling and tasting cheeses in the world are washed rind varieties.

CHEESES A TO Z

ALLGAU EMMENTALER

A German version of Emmentaler made in 98 kg (220 lb) sizes, matured up to eight months.
(See *Emmentaler*.)

ALPKASE

A type of German Emmentaler made in the High Alps. The cheese is also known as Bergkäse.
(See *Emmentaler*.)

ALTAPOL

Country of origin: Australia.

Background: This is a new cheese with a higher than normal level of polyunsaturated fats. The cheese was developed by the Australian Commonwealth Scientific and Industrial Research Organisation and is now marketed by a commercial company. According to the manufacturers, milk usually has a polyunsaturated fat level of three per cent. Altapol has a polyunsaturated fat level of 20 per cent.

The cheese was developed in view of mounting evidence from heart research implicating saturated fats with cardiovascular illness. It is a cheese obviously suitable for anyone with a heart condition or merely concerned with fat intake.

Description: Altapol is a Cheddar style cheese, light yellow in colour with a firm, close texture. It is marketed in 5 kg (11¼ lb) rindless blocks. Processed and smoked process versions are also produced in 250 g (8 oz) packs.

Altapol has a pleasant Cheddar taste, undemanding but not unattractive with a mildish tangy bite.

Wines: Light reds and whites.
Serve: Snacks; sandwiches.
Fat content: 34 per cent.
Aroma: Unpronounced.
Type: Cheddar.

ALTESSE

A French double crème, creamy, rich but essentially mild tasting. The cheese has a 60 per cent fat content and is marketed in a square cardboard box weighing approximately 210 g (7 oz). Used chiefly as a dessert cheese, it goes well with fruit or French bread. The cheese is easily spreadable once it has reached room temperature.
(See *Double Crèmes*.)

AMBROSIA

Country of origin: Sweden.

Description: A popular, widely marketed Swedish cheese usually produced in wheel shapes some 25 cm (10 in) in diameter and some 10 cm (4 in) deep. It has a waxed rind.

The cheese is made from cow's milk and ripened for about two months. It has a semi-soft rather waxy texture, is a light yellow in colour and has a series of small holes and splits across the interior paste. In taste Ambrosia is smooth, creamy and buttery but with a faintly sourish tinge, rather like a very mild Esrom.

Wines: Dry whites, light reds.
Serve: End of meals, snacks.
Fat content: 45 per cent.
Type: Monastery/mild.
Aroma: Unpronounced.

Description: Blue Vinny is a cylindrical cheese standing some 15 cm (6 in) high and 20 cm (8 in) in diameter. Made from skimmed cow's milk, it is a blue veined cheese which develops a single blue streak, rather than a network of veins. The cheese has a noticeable aroma and a sharp pronounced flavour, somewhat salty.

Blue Vinny is matured for up to six months and needs to be eaten fairly promptly, as it is notorious for hardening very quickly once it ages past its prime.

This cheese virtually disappeared from sight when English health regulations decreed that cheesemaking could not take place in buildings where animals were kept. To develop the blue mould in the cheese, the old cheesemakers used to dip horse bridles into the milk. The micro-organisms on the bridles started the mould.

Blue Vinny is now being made again and produced under more controlled conditions, but is still quite rare.

Wines: Full-bodied reds.
Serve: End of meals.
Fat content: Up to 28 per cent.
Type: Blue vein.
Aroma: Noticeable smell of mould.

BODALLA

(See Australian *Cheddars*.)

BOLINA

A Danish blue vein modelled on Gorgonzola. (See *Blue Veins*.)

BONBEL

Country of origin: France.

Background: Bonbel, of fairly recent origin, is a brand name for yet another version of Saint Paulin.

Description: Bonbel is made in disc shapes some 5 cm (2 in) thick and 23 cm (9 in) in diameter. It is a cow's milk cheese which is ripened for two months. Bonbel is light yellow in colour with a smooth, supple-feeling texture and rind. In flavour it could be said to be a mild-mannered Saint Paulin or Port Salut—creamy, buttery-rich and sweet with a light tangy aftertaste. The cheese is often marketed in a yellow plastic case.

Wines: Light whites and reds, nothing too fruity.
Serve: End of meals or as a snack.
Fat content: 50 per cent.
Type: Monastery.
Aroma: Unpronounced.

BONDON

A version of the French soft bloomy rind cheese Neufchâtel. Cheeses of this type have been produced in Normandy for centuries. (See *Neufchâtel*.)

BOULETTE D'AVESNES

Country of origin: France.

Background: This cheese is related to Maroilles. It was formerly a French farm cheese but is now being made by a number of commercial producers.

Description: The cheese is produced in the shape of a small cone, no more than 7.5 cm (3 in) in diameter and 10 cm (4 in) high. It has a natural red-tinted rind and a soft greyish interior. Made from cow's milk, Boulette d'Avesnes is produced by taking flawed Maroilles, mashing them and adding herbs such as parsley, tarragon and pepper. It is then ripened in damp cellars for three months.

To the uninitiated, d'Avesnes has an arresting flavour, to say the least—somewhat reminiscent of an over-ripe continental sausage. Its aroma matches its taste—extremely sharp and pronounced in both smell and flavour—not a cheese for the faint-hearted.

Boulette de Cambrai is a variation made in the shape of a small ball. This cheese does not undergo the three-month ripening period and is pure white in colour with less aroma and strength of flavour than d'Avesnes. Similar herbs are used to flavour it.

Boulette de la Pierre-Qui-Vire is another fresh, unripened variation of this cheese, more aromatic than de Cambrai.

Wines: Full-bodied reds.
Serve: End of meals; snacks.
Fat content: 50 per cent.
Type: Strong smelling/monastery.
Aroma: Pronounced.

BOURSAULT

Country of origin: France.

Background: This is a popular and widely marketed variety of one of the many types of French triple crème cheeses.

Description: Boursault is made in the shape of a small cylinder about 7.5 cm (3 in) in diameter and 5 cm (2 in) thick. Like all triple crèmes it is made from cow's milk enriched with cream. It is creamy off-white in colour and has a very thin, bloomy rind, soft and downy. The more down you see on the outside of the cheese, the older and stronger it is likely to be. Boursault is a very rich tasting cheese, lush, soft and creamy.

Wines: Any dessert wine, traminers, sauternes; alternatively fruity reds.
Serve: With fresh fruit—particularly apples, strawberries or pears; alternatively, sprinkle with pepper and serve with plain cracker biscuits; good with coffee.
Fat content: 75 per cent.
Type: Triple crème.
Aroma: Unpronounced.

BOURSIN

Country of origin: France.

Background: One of the new French triple crème cheeses which have become extremely popular in recent years.

Description: Due to its high cream content, Boursin is not for the diet-conscious. The cheese is often made in the shape of a small cylinder 7.5 cm (3 in) in diameter and 5 cm (2 in) high. It has a high per cent fat content which gives it a buttery texture and exceptional softness.

Boursin can be eaten in its natural state, when it is pure white in colour. French manufacturers, however, have produced several variations by adding aromatic herbs such as rosemary, fennel, chives and garlic. There is also a variety covered with pepper. The cheese itself is mild and rich, like all double and triple crème cheeses. When flavoured with herbs the predominant taste sensation is that of the herb, offset by the rich creaminess of the cheese itself.

Wines: Serve the plain variety with light dry whites, reds and rosés; the fine herb varieties with white burgundy, burgundy; the pepper variety with cabernet sauvignon or vintage port.
Serve: End of meals or as a luxurious and totally self-indulgent snack—with thin biscuits or wafers of crisp apple.
Fat content: 70-75 per cent.
Type: Triple crème.
Aroma: Unpronounced.

BRAIDED CHEESE

This is an Armenian cheese which has become quite popular in the USA. 'Ropes' of the cheese are braided (the ropes are just under 2.5 cm (1 in) in diameter and packaged in 250 g (8 oz) and 500 g (1 lb) packages. The cheese has caraway seeds lightly dispersed through it. Because of its pronounced salty flavour, it is first soaked in water; the cheese can then be pulled apart in strings and eaten as an appetiser.
(See *Spiced Cheeses*.)

BRESCIANO

An Italian Grana cheese used for grating.
(See *Grana* and *Parmesan*.)

Wines: Light reds, dry whites.
Serve: Snacks; an unusual cheese to serve at end of meals sprinkled with black pepper.
Fat content: 45 per cent.
Type: Bland/buttery.
Aroma: Unpronounced.

BUTTER CHEESE

Country of origin: Germany.

Background: This cheese is also known as Damenkäse or 'ladies cheese'. It is a very mild and bland cheese in marked contrast to the German sour curd and skimmed milk varieties.

Description: An extremely undemanding cheese, soft, rich, creamy and bland. It is made in sausage shapes or in the form of small loaves and has a brown to pale red outer skin. Its interior is smooth, free of holes and with the consistency and colour of butter. The cheese is virtually odourless and mild with just a slightly sour quality to its taste.

The Germans put this into the category of semi-soft, sliceable cheeses.

Wines: Light red wines, rosés, light whites.
Serve: End of meals, snacks.
Fat content: 50 per cent.
Type: Bland/buttery.
Aroma: Unpronounced.

CABOC

A double crème Scottish cheese which is rolled in oatmeal. The cheese is made in small log shapes about 10 cm (4 in) in length and weighs approximately 120 g (4 oz).
(See *Double Crèmes*.)

CABRION

A French goat's milk cheese from Burgundy soaked in marc and ripened in fresh husks of newly-pressed grapes.
(See *Chèvres*.)

CACIOCAVALLO

Country of origin: Italy.

Background: This cheese, which comes from the region of Naples, dates back to the Middle Ages. Many theories have been advanced for the origin of its name, which means 'horse cheese'.

One explanation has it that the cheese was once made from mare's milk; another that it was simply named after Monte Cavallo in Italy where it was first made. At one time the cheese was imprinted with a galloping horse—the mark of the kingdom of Naples. *Larousse Gastronomique* states that the name comes from the ripening process, when the cheeses are straddled in pairs over sticks—like packs on a horse.

Caciocavallo is a *pasta filata* variety, so called because the curd is immersed in hot water, and worked into shape by hand while it is easily malleable. As the cheese curd is cut into small pieces during the making process or 'cheddared', Caciocavallo is related to the Cheddar family of cheeses.

Description: Caciocavallo is moulded by hand into a gourd-like shape with a narrow end or 'neck' which allows the cheeses to be roped together in pairs and left to ripen. The cheese, made from cow's milk, measures some 12.5 cm (5 in) in diameter and 40 cm (16 in) in length.

Caciocavallo is dark yellow in colour with an ivory white interior and a firm, smooth-textured body when young.

Young cheeses, which are ripened for about four months, are mild but with a tang tasting rather like a young Cheddar; aged for twelve months or more they acquire a pronounced spicy and salty sharpness and a hard, granular texture. They are then used for grating and cooking. This cheese is a forebear of the popular Italian cooking cheese Provolone. Unlike Provolone, Caciocavallo is not always smoked and has a slightly lower fat content.

Wines: Light fruity reds for young cheeses; heavy red wines for older cheeses.
Serve: Young cheeses can be served at the table with bread, biscuits and fruits such as pineapple, dried apricots and red and green

peppers; aged Caciocavallo is used for grating.
Fat content: 44 per cent.
Type: Extra hard grating cheese/Cheddar.
Aroma: Unpronounced.

CACIOTTA

This is the name given to a large range of Italian country cheeses which are made from cow's, goat's or sheep's milk. They are all simple, unsophisticated rural cheeses usually produced in small sizes and given individual names related to where they are made. Two of the best known are Cacio Fiore and Cacio Fiore Aquilano. They are similar to the stracchino style cheeses—soft, white, mild and delicate tasting. Unlikely to be seen outside Italy.
(See *Stracchino*.)

CAERPHILLY

Country of origin: Great Britain (Wales).

Background: This is one of the nine famous 'champion' cheeses—the traditional English cheeses. It takes its name from Caerphilly, a small town seven miles north of Cardiff. The cheese, which has been eaten there for centuries, has always been a great favourite with the Welsh miners, who would take it with them to the coalface for a lunchtime snack. The miners appreciated Caerphilly's salty tang when working underground, perhaps because its salt content replaced the salt lost through excessive perspiration in the hot and humid conditions of the mines. The miners found, too, that the cheese remained fresh and moist under these conditions.

Description: Caerphilly is a white, mild cheese that takes only two weeks to mature. It is semi-soft, rather flaky in texture with a definite salty flavour. Its mildness makes it easily digestible and the cheese leaves a clean, fresh taste on the palate. Caerphilly has been aptly described as a 'gentle' cheese.

Like the other eight 'champion' cheeses of England, Caerphilly is made in cylindrical shapes weighing up to 4.5 kg (10 lb); in rindless blocks weighing up to 20 kg (45 lb) and is also sold in small vacuum-packed pieces. As with all cheeses, its flavour sharpens with age; Caerphilly bought outside the UK will not be as fresh and will taste altogether less delicate. Its salty tang will be more pronounced and it will develop a noticeable 'bite'.

Wines: Dry madeira, fairly dry sherry, hock or a dry rosé.
Serve: End of meals; as a snack with celery and thin slices of bread and butter.
Fat content: 45 per cent.
Type: Cheddar family.
Aroma: Unpronounced.

CALCAGNO

A Pecorino style hard, grating cheese from Sicily.
(See *Pecorino Romano*.)

CAMEMBERT

Country of origin: France.

Background: One of the world's most famous cheeses—again one created by the French. Camembert comes from Normandy which, as early as the twelfth century, had a reputation as a cheesemaking centre.

A Madame Marie Harel, a farmer's wife, is said to have created Camembert around 1790, although it is more likely that the good lady brought to a final stage of development what was a traditional-style cheese of the area. Whatever the truth of the matter, the cheese became a favourite of Napoleon's and the French put up statues in her honour.

Camembert started on the road to worldwide fame in 1890 when it was first packaged in small cylindrical boxes. Before this, the cheese was traditionally wrapped in straw, which meant that it could not travel long distances without becoming spoiled.

Description: The art of eating Camembert is to get it at what the experts call *à point*—that is, at the optimum peak of ripeness. Take advice from your cheese seller on this, but there are certain checks you can make your-

RUE LEPIC
CAMEMBERT
PRODUCT OF FRANCE
CHABURET
FRANCE
baby camembert
FAT SOFT CHEESE MIN NET WEIGHT 8 OZ PRODUCT OF FRANCE
MEMBERT
de
MANDIE
TELAIN
MATIERE GRASSE
PURCREM
fromage que l'on aime
PURCREM

self. A Camembert in good condition has a slightly off-white 'mouldy' crust covered with fine down and lightly touched with reddish pigmentation. (Camemberts made outside France tend to be whiter.) The interior paste is creamy yellow with a honey-like fluidity that is the same consistency throughout. When the cheese is cut and it is at its peak, this paste will bulge out from beneath its crust in one solid soft mass. The average sized cheese is approximately 11 cm (4½ in) in diameter and 3.75 cm (1½ in) thick.

A ripe Camembert should be supple and will feel tender and springy when squeezed gently across its diameter. The cheese should never be hard, shrunken or excessively pigmented with red mould or smell of ammonia. All these things are signs of an over-aged, over-ripe cheese. An under-ripe cheese will not have the necessary fluid consistency in its interior and may have a hardish chalky mid-section.

Camembert is a cheese that ripens from the outside—that is, it is surface ripened. It develops its 'mouldy' crust as a result of being treated with a *Penicillium* spore. The crust, known as a 'flowery' or 'bloomy' rind because of the delicate mould that grows on its surface, is quite edible, but not when it is dried out and shrunken.

The cheese, which is made from cow's milk, is produced in small flat disc shapes and spends between one and two months ripening before marketing. Camembert has no pronounced aroma, apart from a light, fresh and not unpleasant smell of mould. There are so many different makes of Camembert that its flavour varies considerably. At its best it is delicately mild but with a rich, delicious and creamy tang. Camembert is a cheese which should be eaten at its peak, within a day or so of purchase —it will not keep and quickly passes its prime.

The cheese is produced in countries all over Europe and in countries as far apart as Australia and the USA, but the French varieties, of which there are many, are generally acknowledged as the finest.

Similar style cheeses include Brie, Carré de l'Est and Chaource.

Wines: Claret; light dry whites.
Serve: End of meals; a Camembert served with fresh tomatoes, capsicum, rye bread and a lightly tossed salad makes a delectable lunch; an over-aged Camembert can be coated with raw egg, dipped in breadcrumbs, pan-fried and then served with jam for an arresting and offbeat dessert.
Fat content: 45-50 per cent.
Type: Brie/Camembert family.
Aroma: Unpronounced.

CANESTRATO

Also known as Pecorino Siciliano, this is a sheep's milk cheese which is the Sicilian version of Pecorino Romano. A *canestro* is the draining basket used during the making process; the marks of the basket can be seen on the cheese. A good, fulsome, rustic table cheese; aged versions are used for grating.
(See *Pecorino Romano*.)

CANTAL

Country of origin: France.

Background: One of the oldest of the French cheeses which is believed to date back to Roman days. Cantal is made on the slopes of the Auvergne mountains and is a member of the Cheddar family.

Description: Cantal is a hard, yellow cheese made from cow's milk in cylindrical shapes up to 40 cm (16 in) high and 45 cm (18 in) in diameter. It has a cloth-covered, greyish rind beneath which is a light yellow interior paste, free of holes but sometimes with a few cracks. The interior texture is firm, resilient and supple. Large Cantals can weigh as much as 54 kg (120 lb) but smaller sized cheeses which weigh in the region of 7 kg (16 lb) are made. The cheese, which undergoes a 'cheddaring' process, is ripened for periods varying between three and six months.

In taste, the cheese is similar to a good mature Cheddar, mellow, fulsome but with a rather sweetish, nutty flavour. Older Cantals develop a greater pungency and bite.

Wines: Fruity beaujolais-style reds; also goes with beer.
Serve: A first class all-purpose table cheese.

Australian Camemberts

Fat content: 45 per cent.
Type: Cheddar.
Aroma: Rich milky aroma when cut.

CAPRICE DES DIEUX

Country of origin: France.

Background: A double crème cheese from the Champagne area.

Description: Caprice des Dieux is a Brie/Camembert style double crème cheese. It is matured for several weeks so that it develops the typical bloomy rind of cheeses of this type, pure white flecked with pink-brown pigmentation. The interior paste is cream white, soft, spreadable, rich and buttery. The cheese takes the shape of an oval loaf about 14 cm (5½ in) long, is under 5 cm (2 in) high and weighs around 250 g (8 oz). It is marketed in a cardboard box.

In flavour the cheese, with its high fat content, is like a richer Brie or Camembert, uncomplicated but thick and luscious.

Wines: Fruity reds but also goes with full flavoured whites.
Serve: End of meals with fresh fruit; essentially a dessert cheese.
Fat content: 60 per cent.
Type: Double crème, Brie/Camembert style.
Aroma: Unpronounced.
(See *Double Crèmes*.)

CAPRICETTE

This is a French skimmed goat's milk cheese with a delicate texture and soft, creamy flavour. It is marketed in 90 g (3 oz) plastic cups. A good mild cheese to start with if you're interested in acquiring a taste for goat's milk cheeses.
(See *Chèvres*.)

CAPRINO

Generic term for a range of semi-soft goat's milk cheeses from the Argentine.

CAPRINO ROMANO

The goat's milk version of the Italian grating cheese Pecorino Romano which is made from sheep's milk.
(See *Pecorino Romano*.)

CARRE DE L'EST

Country of origin: France.

Background: This cheese comes from Alsace-Lorraine. Its name means square cheese of the east.

Description: This is a soft, bloomy-rind cheese similar to Camembert. It differs from Camembert in its shape, being made in 10 cm (4 in) squares about 2.5 cm (1 in) thick. The cheese, which is ripened for a three week period, has the familiar downy white or bloomy rind of a Camembert and the creamy ivory-white interior paste. It has a slight mushroomy aroma.

Carré de l'Est is made from cow's milk. In flavour it is reminiscent of Camembert but rather blander and less sophisticated; it can be looked on as an interesting but simpler and milder version of the more famous Normandy cheese. American-made Camemberts are considered to be somewhat similar in taste to Carré de l'Est.

Wines: Light reds and dry whites.
Serve: End of meals; lunch-time snacks.
Fat content: 45-50 per cent.
Type: Camembert/Brie.
Aroma: Unpronounced.
(See *Camembert*.)

CASIGIOLU

A member of the Italian pasta filata (drawn curd) family of cheeses. The best known cheeses of this type are Provolone and Caciocavallo, widely used in cooking for a variety of Italian style dishes.
(See *Pasta Filata* and *Provolone*.)

CENDRES

The name given to a range of French cheeses that are ripened in ashes. They are usually produced in the wine growing areas of France and are unlikely to be seen outside their country of origin.

CHABICHOU

Country of origin: France.

Background: A well rated French *chèvre* from the Poitou province of France produced both commercially and on farms. It is sometimes known as Cabichou, Cabrichiu or Chabi.

Description: Chabichou is a soft, natural rind goat's milk cheese made in a truncated cone shape about 7 cm (2½ in) across and 5 cm (2 in) high. Some are made in rectangle shapes. The farm-produced Chabichous, known as Chabis, have a bluish rind, the factory-made ones a white rind. The cheeses are ripened in dry cellars for about three weeks. They weigh about 90 g (3 oz).

In flavour, Chabichous are decidedly 'goaty', quite pronounced, fruity and intense; farmhouse varieties are usually stronger flavoured than commercially produced ones. Either way, a cheese for those who like a strong flavour; the aroma is equally noticeable.

Wines: Nothing fancy, an inexpensive, fruity red.
Serve: End of meals.
Fat content: 45 per cent.
Type: Goat's milk.
Aroma: Pronouncedly 'goaty'.
(See *Chèvres*.)

CHAOURCE

Another French Camembert style cheese measuring 10 cm (4 in) in diameter and 6 cm (2½ in) high. The cheese has a soft downy white and a rich pale yellow interior. A soft, rich cheese with a mild but fruity taste with a hint of mushrooms in the aroma. The cheese comes from the Champagne area and has a 45-50 per cent fat content.
(See *Camembert*.)

CHAUMES

A French variety of Limburger made in 25 cm (10 in) diameter wheel shapes 2.5 cm (1 in) thick. It has the orange coloured rind familiar to many other cheeses of this type.
(See *Limburger*.)

CHAVIGNOL

A French chèvre, or goat's milk cheese, also known as Crottin de Chavignol. Aged versions of this cheese can be quite overpowering in taste and aroma.
(See *Crottin de Chavignol* and *Chèvres*.)

CHEDDAR

Country of origin: Great Britain (England).

Background: Cheddar, the most popular and widely copied English cheese in the world, originally came from the Cheddar Gorge area in Somerset, where it has been made since the fifteenth century. The cheese gained widespread popularity in Tudor times and formerly was noted for the huge sizes in which it was made. Cheddars weighing 56 kg (126 lb) were commonplace and one made for Queen Victoria's wedding celebrations measured 3 m (9 ft) across. Giant Cheddars are now a thing of the past and fewer are made in the traditional cylindrical shape.

Description: Cheddar is now made all over the world, as far away as America and Australia. Cheddars vary considerably in taste, but the traditional English cheese is rich and nutty tasting with a close, creamy texture. The English put the cheese into two categories: mild, aged up to five months, with a characteristic clean and mellow but not pronounced flavour; and mature, aged eight months or more, a

COMTE

Country of origin: France.

Background: This cheese, which dates back to the thirteenth century, is a French type of Gruyère. It is also known as Gruyère de Comté.

Description: The cheese has a hard, thick outer rind, a brownish yellow in colour, and a smooth, firm-textured pale yellow interior dotted with small holes the size of cherries. Comté is made in the shape of flattened cylindrical wheels up to 65 cm (26 in) in diameter and 10 cm (4 in) thick. It weighs in the region of 40 kg (90 lb).

Like Gruyère, Comté is a cooked, pressed cheese. It is similar in taste to the Swiss cheese, but less sweet, slightly sharper with rather more bite. Its flavour can become quite pronounced with age.

Wines: Light but full grape-flavoured dry whites and reds.
Serve: A good cheese for the cheeseboard at end of meals; it is also an excellent cooking cheese for such dishes as fondues.
Fat content: 45 per cent.
Type: Swiss.
Aroma: Unpronounced.

COON

A highly regarded and quite sharp and pronounced Cheddar from New York State. The cheese is ripened in an atmosphere with a high temperature and high humidity.
(See American *Cheddars.*)

CORNHUSKER

This is an American Cheddar similar to Colby, developed by the Nebraska Agricultural Experiment Station in 1940. It has a softer texture than Cheddar and contains more moisture, and therefore does not keep as long.
(See American *Cheddars.*)

COROLLE DU POITOU

Although from the Poitou region of France, well known for its goat's milk cheeses, this cheese is made from cow's milk. It is a double crème Camembert/Brie style cheese with a 60 per cent fat content. The cheese has a firm centre with creamy edges and a white downy surface.
(See *Double Crèmes.*)

COTHERSTONE

This is a rare Yorkshire cheese sometimes known as Yorkshire Stilton. A blue vein that resembles Stilton, it was first produced in the Tees Valley, Yorkshire, England. Highly considered but extremely hard to come by.

COTSWOLD

Country of origin: Great Britain (England).

Background: This is one of several new varieties of English cheese flavoured with various additives.

Description: Cotswold is a version of the traditional English cheese Double Gloucester with chives added. It has the smooth, mellow taste of the typical Gloucester with the chives imparting a fragrant, delicate, oniony flavour.

Wine: Light reds; also goes well with beer.
Serve: End of meals; lunch with a light salad and beer.
Fat content: 45 per cent.
Type: Cheddar family.
Aroma: Unpronounced.

COTTAGE CHEESE

Country of origin: Unknown.

Background: This fresh, unripened cheese, originally made from naturally soured milk, is one of the oldest forms of cheese known to

man. It was developed before the ripening process was discovered—possibly the accidental result of one of these cheeses being stored and forgotten.

Description: The cheese is simply made by milk being set with a lactic starter, cut, drained of whey and then packed. The cheese is not ripened. In appearance it takes the form of a lumpy white mass made up of small white curd particles.

There are many varieties of Cottage Cheese on the market which differ greatly in the way they are made, their fat content and their flavour. One of the most popular is the American and Australian bland-flavoured curd style, made from skimmed milk.

The curd of American and Australian Cottage Cheese receives repeated washings, which cuts down the acidity of the cheese and results in a flavour bland to very mildly acid. Cream is often added to give the cheese extra moisture and a more attractive flavour. The cheese is usually marketed in plastic containers. Creamed Cottage Cheese is available with flavourings as varied as gherkin and pineapple.

Continental-style Cottage Cheese is often marketed in cellophane or plastic envelopes or sausage-shaped packs. This cheese is not washed during its manufacture and its flavour is therefore sharper and more acid. There is little separation in the cheese and it appears as a solid packed mass. Its chief use lies in cooking.

Cottage Cheese is also known as Pot Cheese, Dutch Cheese and Schmierkäse. In America it is sometimes called Popcorn Cheese—in reference to its curd particles.

In all its forms Cottage Cheese has great appeal to dieters and weight watchers because of its low fat and calorie content.

Varieties can have a fat content of between 4 and 15 per cent, depending on the manufacturer. The Continental-style non-fat Cottage Cheese has up to only 4 per cent fat content.

Wines: Not really applicable, but a light rosé or white wine is a possibility.
Serve: The bland American Cottage Cheese goes with salad vegetables, on open sandwiches or as a base for potato salads or appetisers. Alternatively, it can be served on a dessert platter with fresh fruits such as strawberries,

peaches, melon, grapes or pineapple. The sharper flavour of Continental Cottage Cheese makes it less popular in salads and sweet dishes, but is often used in cheesecakes, savoury or dessert soufflés, fillings for pancakes, cannelloni or lasagne dishes or as a base for dips and spreads.
Fat content: Varies between 4-15 per cent.
Type: Fresh, unripened.
Aroma: Unpronounced.

COULOMMIERS

Country of origin: France.

Background: This cheese can be considered a small-sized version of Brie. It takes its name from the town in the Seine et Marne region where it is made.

Description: Coulommiers is a soft, disc-shaped cheese 12.5 cm (5 in) in diameter and 2.5 cm (1 in) thick, made from cow's milk. It is very similar in appearance to Brie, having a downy white, bloomy rind and a soft, creamy yellow, loosely flowing interior. The cheese has a pleasantly fresh bouquet and the delectable rich, creamy, fruity Brie-type flavour.

Coulommiers is ripened for a four-week period. As with all cheeses of this type, it will not keep and should be eaten soon after purchase. Larger versions of this cheese measuring 25 cm (10 in) in diameter are known as Brie de Coulommiers.

Wines: Light but fruity reds.
Serve: End of meals.
Fat content: 45-50 per cent.
Type: Camembert/Brie.
Aroma: Unpronounced.
(See *Brie*.)

CREAM CHEESE

Country of origin: Unknown.
Background: Like Cottage Cheese, this is one of the most ancient forms of cheese in the world. An English version known as Slipcote was extremely popular in Shakespeare's time. Mrs Beaton did not think it should be classed

Cottage Cheeses and Creamed Cottage Cheeses

as a cheese at all. She wrote: 'Cream cheese, although so-called, is not properly cheese, but is nothing more than cream dried sufficiently to be cut with a knife.'

Description: Cream Cheese is a soft, rich, fresh unripened cheese made in a similar fashion to Cottage Cheese. The main difference is that Cream Cheese is made from milk and cream, which is added after the whey has been drained from the milk-curd. This results in a soft, white, rindless smooth-textured mass of cheese with a rich and mildly acid flavour. The cheese is usually marketed foil-wrapped, in tubs or plastic containers.

The term 'cream cheese' is also used more generally in reference to double and triple crème cheeses (cheeses with an exceptionally high fat content) and soft, bloomy rind cheeses such as Neufchâtel. These are very different types of cream cheese and should not be confused with the cheese under discussion here.

Wines: A light rosé; alternatively coffee or tea.
Serve: Fresh Cream Cheese is used in cheesecakes, gelatine-based desserts and savoury snacks. It can also be used in dips, served with dry biscuits, dried fruits, carrot and celery sticks, cucumber wedges, pretzels or pressed fruits. It is an excellent base for dessert and savoury cooking and can be delicious with seasonal fresh fruits as a whipped creamy topping.
Fat content: 35-38 per cent.
Type: Fresh, unripened.
Aroma: Unpronounced.

CREMA DANIA

Country of origin: Denmark.

Background: This cheese, which first appeared in the late 1950s, was the creation of one Henrik Tholstrup of Copenhagen. In many ways it is similar to Brie but has a much higher fat content.

Description: Crema Dania is made from cow's milk enriched with cream. The cheese is made in rectangular bar shapes weighing about 180 g (6 oz) and comes foil-wrapped in a cardboard box. The cheese has a thin bloomy white rind developed after a three-week ripening period, and a smooth, yellow-white interior. The interior paste is creamy and soft, very easy to spread. The cheese ripens very evenly and when at its best has a rich gloss. In taste, the cheese is Brie-like, very rich, creamy, smooth and delectable. It is considered one of Denmark's most notable contributions to the cheese world. Crema Dania's high fat content makes it a double crème cheese, almost a triple crème.

A similar cheese, also Danish, is Crème Royale.

Wines: Light reds; dry whites; light rosés.
Serve: Serve as a dessert with fruits such as strawberries.
Fat content: 72 per cent.
Type: Double crème.
Aroma: Unpronounced.

CREME CHERRY

Brand name for a Norwegian processed cheese range.
(See *Processed Cheese.*)

CREME DE GRUYERE

A French range of processed cheese.
(See *Processed Cheese.*)

CREME DE SAVOIE

A French range of processed cheese.
(See *Processed Cheese.*)

CREME ROYALE

A Danish double crème cheese similar to Crema Dania.
(See *Crema Dania.*)

CREOLE

An American Cottage style cheese enriched with cream, made in Louisiana and popular in New Orleans.
(See *Cottage* and *Cream Cheese*.)

CRESCENZA

This is an Italian stracchino-style cheese. These cheeses are chiefly soft, white and virtually rindless, are designed to be eaten fresh—they are ripened for periods of only ten to fifteen days. Consequently such cheeses are usually so fresh and delicate that they rarely leave Italy. Crescenza is one of the most highly rated—a very rich, full white creamy cheese, so soft textured it can be spread like butter.
(See *Stracchino*.)

CROTTIN DE CHAVIGNOL

A French chèvre or goat's milk cheese from the Berry province with quite a ferocious reputation. These cheeses have a bloomy natural rind, brownish to dark grey depending on age. They are made in the shape of small 60 g (2 oz) balls. The interiors are soft and cream white when young but darken as they mature. Such cheeses are matured for between two weeks and up to three months. The traditional aged cheeses are extremely pungent and powerful in taste; their aroma is correspondingly rank—most certainly an acquired taste. The young cheeses are, of course, far milder. This cheese is also known as Chavignol from the town where it is made. Crottin simply means 'horse dung'—it refers to the appearance of the cheese, not its taste! (Although people unmoved by its charms might not agree.)
(See *Chèvres*.)

CUMIN CHEDDAR

A flavoured natural Cheddar cheese made in Queensland and South Australia, this is a smooth, firm bodied semi-matured Cheddar with spicy, whole cumin seeds adding a richly piquant flavour.
(See *Cheddar*.)

DAISY

(See American *Cheddars*.)

DAMENKASE

A very mild and bland cheese more commonly known as Butter Cheese. The name means 'ladies' cheese'.
(See *Butter Cheese*.)

DANABLU

Country of origin: Denmark.

Background: Also known as Danish Blue, this is one of the most widely distributed Danish blue-veined cheeses. Danablu is modelled on the French Roquefort, although it is made from cow's milk rather than ewe's milk. The other internationally marketed Danish blue vein is Mycella, a copy of Gorgonzola.

Description: Full size, Danablu generally appears as a flat, cylindrical cheese weighing 2.5-3 kg (6-7 lb) with a diameter of 20 cm (8 in) and a height of 10 cm (4 in). It is also made in rectangular and square shapes.

Consumer portions are marketed in 125 g (¼ lb), 250 g (½ lb) and 30 g (1 oz) pieces, wrapped in foil or clear film. The cheese is also supplied in circular and rectangular plastic cups containing 125-250 g (¼-½ lb). Danablu has a thin, white to yellowish-white, slightly greasy surface and a creamy-white interior with delicate blue veining, the result of inoculation with the *Penicillium roqueforti* spore. It is soft-textured, with a creamy consistency, being both spreadable and sliceable. Danablu is, however, a stronger-tasting blue vein than its companion Mycella, having a sharp, distinctive, piquant flavour, sometimes over-salty.

Wines: Red wines, clarets, burgundies.
Serve: Danablu can be used as a dessert cheese, served with blue grapes or walnuts; in salads or as a cocktail snack on a small square of rye bread with a grape or walnut.
Fat content: 50 per cent (minimum).
Type: Blue vein.
Aroma: Unpronounced, slight smell of mould.

DANBO

Country of origin: Denmark.

Background: This cheese is a member of the Danish family of Samsoe cheeses, Denmark's most popular cheese type. It used to be known as Danish Steppe cheese.

Description: Danbo, made from cow's milk, is made in a flat square measuring 25 cm by 25 cm (10 in) by 7.5 cm (3 in) thick. The rind is dry and yellowish and is sometimes covered with a red or yellow coloured wax.

Danbo has a firm, supple texture with a limited number of small and regularly shaped holes. It is mild, bland and buttery to the taste, faintly sweetish and nut-like. Its flavour sharpens with age. The cheese is usually marketed after maturing for up to five months. Danbo is also made with caraway seeds when it is known as King Christian IX. A Danbo with a 20 per cent fat content is available and is one of the most popular low fat cheeses sold outside Denmark.

Wines: Light whites and reds; beer; also cider.
Serve: A good all-purpose table cheese. Children like it because of its mildness.
Fat content: 45 per cent.
Type: Bland/buttery.
Aroma: Unpronounced.

DANISH CHEF

A range of Danish processed cheese in flavourings varying from shrimp to horseradish.
(See *Processed Cheese*.)

DANISH FONTINA

A Danish copy of the Italian cheese Fontina. The cheese has a red wax rind (unlike the Italian).
(See *Fontina*.)

DANISH SAINT PAULIN

A mild flavoured cheese originally modelled on the French Port Salut. The Danish version is creamy and buttery but less sweet than the French and has a sharper tang.
(See *Port Salut* and *Saint Paulin*.)

DAUPHIN

A version of Maroilles—a strong smelling and pungent tasting French washed rind cheese.
(See *Maroilles*.)

DELICE DE SAINT-CYR

A French triple crème cheese made in 12 cm (5 in) disc shapes just over 2.5 cm (1 in) thick. The cheese is matured for three weeks and develops a light white rind which can be spotted with reddish pigmentation. The cheese has a fat content of 75 per cent, giving it an extremely rich, luscious and creamy flavour with a slight undertone of nuts.
(See *Triple Crèmes*.)

DEMI-SEL

Country of origin: France.

Background: A fresh, unripened cheese from Normandy, similar to Petit Suisse. However, it has a lower fat content and a little salt is added to it. The name refers to its low salt content.

flavour considerably, but all are strong, rich, creamy and pungent tasting cheeses, more creamy and less salty than most other blues. They also have a noticeably pungent aroma.

Wines: Full-bodied reds, ports, heavy red burgundies; if you are lucky enough to encounter a young Gorgonzola, try it with a dry traminer/riesling-style white and crisp apples.
Serve: End of meals with fruit, especially apples or pears; in a crunchy wholegrain brown bread sandwich with slices of apple as part of the filling; as a salad dressing; grilled in hot jacket potatoes; as a topping for a charcoal steak.
Fat content: 48-50 per cent.
Type: Blue vein.
Aroma: Pungent and full.

GOUDA

Country of origin: Holland.

Background: More than half of the Netherlands' cheese production is given over to Gouda—one of the two best-known Dutch cheeses in the world (the other is Edam). It takes its name from the town where it originated in the thirteenth century.

Description: Goudas are made in the shape of small wheels with rounded sides and flat tops and bottoms. They come in various sizes, one of the most common being 35 cm (14 in) in diameter and 10-12.5 cm (4-5 in) thick.
The cheese has a waxed red or yellow rind. The interior is straw-yellow, firm-feeling to the touch, its surface dotted with small and unevenly-shaped holes. Gouda is a mild-tasting cheese, pleasantly creamy and buttery.
Spiced Gouda is a variety flavoured with cumin seed, which makes it quite tangy. It also has a firmer texture.
Dutch Mature Gouda has undergone a longer maturing process of up to a year (normal Goudas are matured for between three to four months) and is noticeably different in taste and appearance. The rind is a darker yellow, almost brown, and the dryness of the rind can extend a good half-inch into the cheese. Mature Gouda has a quite pronounced, distinctive aftertaste, cloying to

the palate and resembling a mild, unsalted Cheddar.
There are also smoked and salt-free versions of Gouda.
'Baby' Goudas are made in weights varying from 310 g (10 oz) to 620 g (20 oz).
In the USA the term 'fresh' Gouda is used to denote the young Goudas as opposed to the mature ones—even though the 'fresh' Goudas have been matured for between three and four months.

Wines: Gouda blends pleasantly with almost any wine and you can also drink beer with it—a cheese for all seasons. The spiced variety is better suited to heavy-bodied reds such as cabernet sauvignon and shiraz styles, and dry rather than sweet whites.
Serve: A good bland all-purpose table cheese —try it with pickles or jam.
Fat content: 48 per cent.
Type: Bland/buttery.
Aroma: Unpronounced.

GOURMANDISE

A widely marketed and popular brand of French processed cheese.
(See *Processed Cheese*.)

GOURNAY

Another name for a type of Neufchâtel—a small, soft, bloomy rind cream cheese which has been made in Normandy for centuries.
(See *Neufchâtel*.)

GRADDOST

Country of origin: Sweden.

Background: Gräddost means 'butter cheese' in Swedish and is essentially a bland and buttery style cheese with a high fat content which relates it to double crèmes.

Description: This is a popular, mass marketed Swedish cheese made in varying sizes in cylinder shapes and rectangular blocks. The cheese has a waxed or paraffined yellow rind with an open textured interior dotted with small, irregularly shaped holes. Gräddost is matured for some two months and is firm textured, supple and easily sliced. It has a fresh, clean, buttery taste, smooth and mild.

Wines: Light reds and whites; goes with beer.
Serve: A good all-purpose snack cheese; blends well with fruit.
Fat content: 60 per cent.
Type: Bland and buttery (its high fat content also puts it in the category of double crèmes).
Aroma: Unpronounced.

GRANA

Country of origin: Italy.

Background: Grana is not one cheese, but several. The name refers to a group of hard, granular Italian cheeses developed about A.D. 1200 in the Po Valley.

Description: All Grana cheeses have in common a hard granular texture, a sharp, biting, pronounced flavour and excellent keeping qualities, even in hot climates. This type of cheese also travels well, which helps make it one of Italy's major cheese export items.
   Grana cheese is principally used for grating. The oldest and best-known member of the group is Parmesan. Grana cheeses are often made in thick wheel shapes up to 45 cm (18 in) in diameter. Their colour is straw-yellow but they are often coated with a blackish mixture of oil and umber.
   Varieties include Lombardo, Lodigiano, Emiliano and Asiago.
   Grana cheeses can be aged for up to four years, which makes them extremely hard and brittle, ideal for grating, but young cheeses (aged under a year) can be used as table cheeses.

Wines: Any full-bodied red such as Chianti.
Serve: Grated onto dishes such as spaghetti bolognaise and minestrone.
Fat content: Approximately 30-35 per cent.

Type: Extra hard grating cheeses.
Aroma: Unpronounced.
(See *Parmesan*.)

GRANA PADANO

One of the numerous range of Italian Grana cheeses of the same *genre* as Parmesan. The cheese is made in large cylinders and can weigh up to 40 kg (16 lb). It has a hard, granular texture and a fragrant, delicate flavour. Such cheeses can be aged up to two years and are widely used for grating. Younger versions can be used as table cheeses. The cheese has a relatively low fat content of 32 per cent.
(See *Parmesan*.)

GRAND VATEL

A French triple crème cheese similar to Délice de Saint-Cyr.
(See *Double Crèmes*.)

GRAPPE

This is a popular French processed cheese distinguished by the fact that grape skins and pips form its rind. In the USA it is known as Grappe but its correct name is La Grappe.
(See *Processed Cheese*.)

GREEN CHEESE

More commonly known as Sapsago, the Swiss grating cheese. It is sometimes called Green Cheese because of its colour.
(See *Sapsago*.)

GRUNLAND

A German range of processed cheeses.
(See *Processed Cheese*.)

Gruyère

GRUYERE

Country of origin: Switzerland.

Background: Next to Emmentaler, Gruyère is Switzerland's best known and most widely exported cheese. It is very old, some authorities believing it to date back to the twelfth century. It takes its name from the valley of Gruyère in the Canton of Fribourg.

Description: Gruyère is similar to Emmentaler but is made in smaller sizes and has a stronger flavour. It is usually made in large wheels measuring just over 75 cm (30 in) in diameter and 10 cm (4 in) thick. Gruyères can weigh between 35-40 kg (78-90 lb).

    Like Emmentaler it is a hard, cooked pressed cheese. Gruyère has a hard outer rind the texture of pressed biscuits and a firm but supple interior, light yellow to amber in colour, scattered with small holes caused by expanding gases released by bacterial growth during the curing process.

    The holes, or 'eyes' as they are sometimes known, are much smaller than those found in Emmentaler. In Gruyère the holes vary between pea and cherry stone size. The cheese takes about six months to ripen, sometimes longer.

    Gruyère's taste varies with its age but, like Emmentaler, it is nut-flavoured, with a sweetish lingering aftertaste, but sharper, more acid and slightly saltier. As Gruyère has a higher fat content, it is also a richer, creamier-tasting cheese than Emmentaler.

    The older the cheese the fuller, deeper and richer tasting it will be.

Wines: Aged dry whites or dry reds such as cabernet sauvignons.
Serve: End of meals as a table cheese; in fondues, quiches, as a surface topping for dishes such as veal cordon bleu and onion soup.
Fat content: 48 per cent.
Type: Swiss.
Aroma: Noticeable smell of nuts.

GRUYERE DE BEAUFORT

An ancient French cheese similar to Gruyère but richer and more buttery tasting. This cheese is more commonly known as Beaufort. (See *Beaufort*.)

GRUYERE DE COMTE

A type of French Gruyère which dates back to the thirteenth century. The cheese is more commonly known as Comté.
(See *Comté*.)

HALOUMY

Country of origin: Greece.

Background: This cheese, found in many parts of the Mediterranean area, is related to Feta. Like Feta, it is a so-called 'pickled' cheese, being matured in brine.

Description: Haloumy appears as a firmish, putty-like mass, creamy white in colour and with a string-like consistency to its texture. When it is made the curd is dipped in hot whey, kneaded, rolled out and folded with mint leaves or herbs between the layers. It is matured in brine which gives it a sharp salty tang; this is usually not as pronounced as in Feta, the mint flavouring the cheese acquires offsetting the sharpness of the salt.

Wines: Fruity reds or Greek wines like Retsina and Ouzo.
Serve: Haloumy can be used in a variety of ways to add a slightly unusual flavouring; in salads, pastries or on a grilled steak; also eaten fondue-style by being dipped into hot water and drawn out in strings.
Fat content: 40 per cent.
Type: Sheep's milk.
Aroma: Unpronounced.

HAND

Country of origin: USA.

Background: This cheese is the American descendant of a type originally made in several European countries and particularly popular

LEICESTER

Country of origin: Great Britain (England).

Background: This used to be one of England's most popular cheeses until it fell out of favour at the end of the 1930s. In recent years Leicester has made a comeback but not to the extent of being classed as the second best cheese in England—a position it once held.

Description: Leicester is a rich deep orange coloured cheese that looks particularly striking on a cheese board. It gets its colouring from the use of an annatto dye, like Cheshire and Double Gloucester. Leicester is matured for a minimum period of ten to twelve weeks. The cheese has a higher moisture content than Cheddar, which means a shorter life span and a softer body. Fully ripe at six months, it is past its prime at one year. It is a loose-textured cheese, rather flaky, with a clean-tasting, creamy, mellow flavour which could be described as medium-strong. The cheese leaves a lingering rich mellow aftertaste on the palate.

Like the other traditional English cheeses it is made in large cylindrical shapes weighing up to 20 kg (45 lb) and is also marketed in rindless blocks or small vacuum-packed pieces. Leicester melts quickly, making it good for toasting.

Wines: Light red wines; beer and cider.
Serve: End of meals, in sandwiches; a good snack cheese; try it with spring onions.
Fat content: 45 per cent.
Type: Cheddar family.
Aroma: Unpronounced.

L'EXPLORATEUR

A French triple crème cheese made in cylinder shapes some 5 cm (2 in) high and 7.5 cm (3 in) in diameter. The cheese is ripened for three weeks during which it develops a delicate, white bloomy rind. Its interior paste is thick, rich and creamy—a texture that is more than matched by its luxurious flavour. The cheese has a 75 per cent fat content.
(See *Triple Crèmes*.)

LEYDEN

Country of origin: Holland.

Background: A traditional spiced cheese formerly produced on farms in the north-western area of the Zuid Holland province. The cheese is stamped with two crossed keys, the symbol of the university city of Leyden.

Description: Leyden is a firm-textured cheese with a semi-hard dark-yellow rind covered with red wax. The cheese is flavoured with caraway and cumin seeds which are scattered through its light yellow interior paste. Leyden is made in cylindrical shapes approximately 40 cm (16 in) in diameter and some 7.5 cm (3 in) thick. Such cheeses can weigh up to 10 kg (22 lb). In taste Leyden is tangy and spicy, nutty and tasty—one of the better spiced cheeses. Two versions are made; one from whole cow's milk and one from skimmed cow's milk. This factor affects the fat content of the cheese.

Nokkelost is the Norwegian version of Leyden (*nokkelost* means 'key' cheese). It is made in cylindrical shapes or rectangular blocks. Although a copy, it tastes quite unlike Leyden. As well as being spiced with caraway and cumin seeds, cloves are also added. It is milder than Leyden, spicy but rather sweeter, softer and more buttery.

Wines: Leyden, fruity red wines, dry whites; the Dutch recommend it with gin; Nokkelost would go with a medium sherry, blanquette, semillon or white burgundies.
Serve: Good sandwich and snack cheeses blending well with tomatoes, cucumber and lettuce; end of meals.
Fat content: 20-40 per cent.
Type: Spiced.
Aroma: Leyden is noticeably spicy; Nokkelost smells of cloves.

LIEDERKRANZ

Country of origin: USA.

Background: Liederkranz came into being towards the end of last century when a New

York cheesemaker attempted to copy a popular German cheese called Bismark Schlosskäse. He succeeded in creating Liederkranz—a cheese with a character entirely of its own and one of the few cheeses considered to be genuine American originals. Liederkranz takes its name from a German singing society to which the cheesemaker belonged; it means 'wreath of song'.

Description: Liederkranz is made in small oblong loaves weighing around 120 g (4 oz). It is a soft, surface-ripened cheese made from cow's milk which is matured for three to four weeks. The cheese has a thin, light orange rind and pale yellow interior, very soft and spreadable and of an almost honey-like consistency when ripe. It has a full and pungent aroma but despite this in taste it is not as strong as one might expect—full flavoured and pungent but rather delicate, rich and distinctive at the same time.

Liederkranz comes foil-wrapped and does not have a long life. It is important to get the cheese at its peak before it becomes over-aged.

Wines: Goes extremely well with beer.
Serve: At end of meals; as a snack on dark bread with beer.
Fat content: 50 per cent.
Type: Strong smelling monastery style.
Aroma: Full and distinctive.

LIMBURGER

Country of origin: Belgium.

Background: This cheese is made in several European countries and is so popular in Germany that it is often thought to have originated there. In fact it was first produced in the Middle Ages by monks in the province of Limburg in Belgium. It is one of the world's most famous 'smelly' cheeses.

Description: Limburger is made from cow's milk, usually in rectangular shapes 15 cm (6 in) long by 7.5 cm (3 in) wide and high. Smaller cube-shaped sizes are also made. The cheese is semi-soft, supple feeling with the smooth, thin, reddish to brownish rind which is a feature of this type of washed rind cheese.

Limburger is surface ripened in a humid atmosphere for three months and has a smooth-textured yellow interior with a few holes, small and irregular in size. The cheese is usually marketed wrapped in foil.

Limburger is distinguished by its powerful odour, very strong and rank—and for many people quite overpowering. Its taste is not as bad (or as good, depending on your point of view) as its smell, but it is still a memorably tangy, pungent and gamy tasting cheese.

American Limburger is usually somewhat milder than the European varieties, which can also tend to get a trifle over-ripe by the time they reach their overseas destination—enhancing their strength even further.

Wines: Full-bodied reds; in Germany it is often eaten with beer.
Serve: As a snack on dark breads with strong-flavoured vegetables like onions, radishes and shallots.
Fat content: 30-40 per cent.
Type: Strong smelling/monastery.
Aroma: Pronounced.

LIPTAUER

A Hungarian cheese from the Province of Liptow, from which the cheese takes its name. It is an unusual cheese in that it is designed to be eaten with a variety of flavouring agents throughout its body; these include paprika, capers, chives, garlic, onions, hot peppers or finely chopped olives. The cheese itself, made from sheep's milk, is soft, faintly oily and has the familiar granular, gritty sheep's milk cheese texture. It is not a particularly strong cheese; the ingredients used to flavour it provide its appeal—a sort of cheese-type smorgasbord.

LIVAROT

Country of origin: France.

Background: An old Normandy cheese noted for both strong taste and strong smell. Versions

Liederkranz (photo courtesy Borden Foods)

of this type of cheese have been made in Normandy since the thirteenth century.

Description: Livarot is a soft, washed rind cheese, surface ripened in humid cellars for three months to allow full bacterial development. It is made from cow's milk in the shape of small discs up to 12.5 cm (5 in) in diameter and 5 cm (2 in) thick.

Like all cheeses of this kind, its rind is smooth, with a glossy finish which varies in colour from reddish-brown to dark brown. The interior paste is cream yellow; when fully ripe Livarot is soft textured to the point when it could almost be spread. After manufacture the cheese is wrapped around with a band of five reeds. It was this practice that caused it to be known as a 'Five-Striper' or 'Livarot-Colonel' in France.

The military reference is quite apt; there is nothing half-hearted about a Livarot. The cheese has a highly developed taste, very strong, spicy and tangy, and well-matched by its powerful odour, which many people find somewhat overpowering.

Wines: Strong, full-bodied reds, port or sherry.
Serve: End of meals; snacks.
Fat content: 40-45 per cent.
Type: Monastery/strong smelling.
Aroma: Pronounced.

LOAF

This is simply the name given to several types of cheese that are made in a rectangular loaf shape. Formerly, most cheeses of this type were processed, but there has been an increasing trend to make more and more natural cheeses ranging from Cheddar to Emmental in rindless rectangular blocks.

LODIGIANO

An Italian grating cheese of the Grana style. The most famous cheese of this type is Parmesan.
(See *Grana* and *Parmesan*.)

LOMBARDO

A Grana style Italian grating cheese, sometimes also called Lombardy. The best known cheese of this type is Parmesan.
(See *Grana* and *Parmesan*.)

LONGHORN

An American Cheddar so called because of its tall conical shape. Its flavour varies from mild to robust depending on age.
(See *Cheddar*.)

LUCULLUS

A French triple crème cheese made in the shape of a small cylinder 7.5 cm (3 in) in diameter and 5 cm (2 in) high. A soft textured cheese with a light bloomy surface rind, slightly pink in colour. Lucullus is a thickly rich creamy cheese with a lightly nutty flavour. It has a fat content of 75 per cent.
(See *Triple Crèmes*.)

MACONNAIS

A square shaped French goat's milk cheese.
(See *Chèvres*.)

MACROBERTSON

(See Australian *Cheddars*.)

MAGNUM

A French double crème cheese which is ripened for a three week period and develops a light bloomy rind. The interior is rich, luscious and creamy. The cheese has a 72 per cent fat content.
(See *Double Crèmes*.)

MAINLAND

(See New Zealand *Cheddars*.)

MAINZ

Country of origin: Germany.

Background: A member of the family of German skimmed sour milk cheeses. It takes its name from an important port on the Rhine. Mainz is related to Harz cheese. Both have a high protein content and a low fat content and are noted for their powerful flavour and aroma.

Description: This cheese is essentially the same as Harz. It is made in small, rubbery discs about 5 cm (2 in) in diameter and 2.5 cm (1 in) thick. The smooth surface may be golden yellow to reddish-brown; the interior is a pale glassy yellow.

These little cheeses possess a very pungent taste and odour and while they range in degree of sharpness of flavour even the milder versions would be found extremely potent by the uninitiated.

Wines: Often eaten with beer; sometimes with cider.
Serve: Snacks.
Fat content: Less than 10 per cent.
Type: Strong smelling.
Aroma: Pronounced.
(See *Harz* and *Sour Curd Cheeses*.)

MALAKOFF

A small, soft, bloomy rind cream cheese which weighs between 100 g and 250 g (4-8 oz). The cheese is essentially a version of the more famous Neufchâtel, considered one of the oldest of the Normandy cheeses.
(See *Neufchâtel*.)

MANCHEGO

Country of origin: Spain.

Description: This is Spain's most popular

and one of its oldest cheeses. It is made from sheep's milk in large cylinder shapes and is matured for about one month. The cheese has a hard yellow natural rind with a firmish textured interior paste varying in colour from white to yellow, sometimes with, sometimes without holes.

At its best an excellent sheep's milk cheese, full flavoured and rich tasting with a distinctive 'sheepy' tang.

Wines: Fruity reds.
Serve: End of meals; snacks.
Fat content: 57 per cent.
Type: Sheep's milk.
Aroma: Noticeable sheepy aroma.

MANTECA

An unusual pasta filata style Italian cheese that is made and looks like a small, rounded Caciocavallo but has in its heart a knob of butter (usually sweet whey butter). Cut open, the Manteca presents a striking combination of texture and colour: the outer part of the cheese, usually smoked, being yellow-brown, while the egg of butter within is a straw yellow colour. This cheese is also known as Burrino. It has a mild, sweet buttery flavour.
(See *Burrino*.)

MAORI GOUDA

This New Zealand cheese tastes quite different to the famous Dutch cheese on which it is based. Maori Gouda is a strong yellow in colour; while initially bland tasting it has a pronounced aftertaste that is reminiscent of sour milk, almost tobacco-like.
(See *Gouda*.)

MARGOTIN

A French double crème cheese available with a covering of pepper or flavoured with herbs. A

cheese with a 60 per cent fat content—rich, creamy and tangy.
(See *Double Crèmes*.)

MARIBO

Country of origin: Denmark.

Background: Maribo is another member of the numerous Danish Samsoe family.

Description: Maribo is a golden wheel-shaped cheese with rounded sides and edges, measuring 43 cm (17 in) in diameter. Whole cheeses weigh in the region of 13 kg (30 lb).

The cheese has a thin, dry, yellow rind and a rich yellow interior, compact and firm-textured with a large number of small, irregular, rice-sized holes spread across it. The holes are quite close together and uniformly spaced.

Maribo undergoes three to four months' maturing which results in a clean taste, bland and mild but just faintly acidulous; it has a noticeable aftertaste, rather like a lighter flavoured Havarti. Aged versions can develop a bitter-sweet aftertaste.

Versions of this cheese, which is made from cow's milk, are also made in rectangular shapes, with or without rinds.

Wines: Light dry whites; medium strength reds, rosés.
Serve: An all-purpose Danish table cheese; goes well with vegetables such as radishes, tomatoes, green peppers and celery.
Fat content: 45 per cent.
Type: Bland/buttery.
Aroma: Unpronounced.

MAROILLES

Country of origin: France.

Background: This cheese was developed by monks at the monastery of Maroilles in the tenth century. The French refer to it as Vieux Puant—Old Stinker.

Description: Maroilles is a soft, washed-rind cheese, powerful in both aroma and flavour. It is made in squares of about 12.5 cm (5 in), and 7.5 cm (3 in) thick. The reddish-brown rind is smooth and shiny, the result of the continual washings the cheese receives during its curing process. The yellow interior paste is semi-firm and supple; when ripe quite soft. During its four month ripening period, the cheese is regularly brushed and bathed in beer.

Maroilles is one of the best-known French 'smelly' cheeses, with an extremely strong bouquet and gamy, tangy, potent flavour. It is made in several shapes and sizes, versions of it being known as Quart, Larron, Boulette, Dauphin and Sorbais.

Wines: Strong, full-bodied reds.
Serve: End of meals with crusty bread; snacks.
Fat content: 45-50 per cent.
Type: Monastery/strong smelling.
Aroma: Pronounced.

MASCARPONE

Country of origin: Italy.

Background: Originally from Lombardy, now made all over Italy, Mascarpone is made from fresh cream, usually in the winter months.

Description: In appearance Mascarpone resembles clotted cream, and appears as a soft white mass usually packaged in plastic tubs and containers. It is a cheese with a high fat content and some authorities challenge whether it should be considered a cheese or a cream. At any rate, all find it delectable—very soft, rich, creamy and buttery in flavour, somewhat like whipped cream, in fact. In Italy it is often sold in muslin bags with sweetened fruits.

When aged Mascarpone develops a firmer texture and a buttery colour and is used for grating.

Wines: Light whites of the style of moselle, traminer and auslese, or a delicate sweet moscato wine.
Serve: Usually eaten as a dessert with sugar and fruit; goes excellently with fruit as varied as strawberries and watermelon. Sometimes mixed with brandy or liqueurs.
Fat content: 60 per cent.
Type: Unripened double crème.
Aroma: Unpronounced.

MATURE EDAM

A Dutch Edam cheese which has been matured for up to one year (Edams are normally matured for between three and four months). Mature Edam is therefore a much stronger tasting cheese—harder and drier and slightly more salty in flavour.
(See *Edam*.)

MATURE GOUDA

A version of Dutch Gouda that has been matured for up to a year. This makes a much stronger tasting cheese with a pronounced and distinctive aftertaste. The rind is a darker yellow than with normal Goudas which are matured for between three and four months.
(See *Gouda*.)

MEJETTE

A whey, Cottage style cheese, the best known version of which is Ricotta.
(See *Ricotta*.)

MIDDEBARE

This is simply the name of the largest sized Edam that the Dutch produce. The cheese can weigh up to 6 kg (14 lb).
(See *Edam*.)

MILANO

A stracchino type Italian cheese sometimes called Stracchino di Milano. Milano is a soft, fast ripening (it is left to mature for only 20 days) table cheese made in Lombardy; mild, sweet and rich tasting—a stracchino *dolce* rather than *piccante*. It can be compared to Bel Paese and Crescenza.
(See *Stracchino* and *Bel Paese*.)

MILKANA

Brand name for a processed Emmentaler cheese range.
(See *Processed Cheese*.)

MIMOLETTE

Country of origin: Holland.

Background: This cheese is widely made in France and though often considered French, is in fact Dutch, and related to Edam and Gouda.

Description: Mimolette is a particularly striking and attractive cheese. Made in a spherical shape about 17.5 cm (7 in) in diameter and 12.5 cm (5 in) high, it is coloured a bright, glowing orange by the use of annatto dye. The cheese has a wax-covered, thin, natural rind and a firm, supple-textured interior usually free of holes.

Mimolette is cured for a minimum period of six months and is made from cow's milk. It is a clean, uncomplicated cheese tasting slightly nutty, rather salty—something like a mature Gouda in flavour and texture.

French Mimolette is similar but rather softer in texture and creamier.

Wines: Light reds; rosés; beer.
Serve: A tasty snack and sandwich cheese; its colour makes it look striking on a cheese board.
Fat content: 45 per cent.
Type: Bland/buttery.
Aroma: Unpronounced.

MINI ESROM

A small-sized version of the Danish cheese Esrom. The mini version is made in a rectangular brick shape weighing between 250 g and 500 g ($\frac{1}{2}$-1 lb).
(See *Esrom*.)

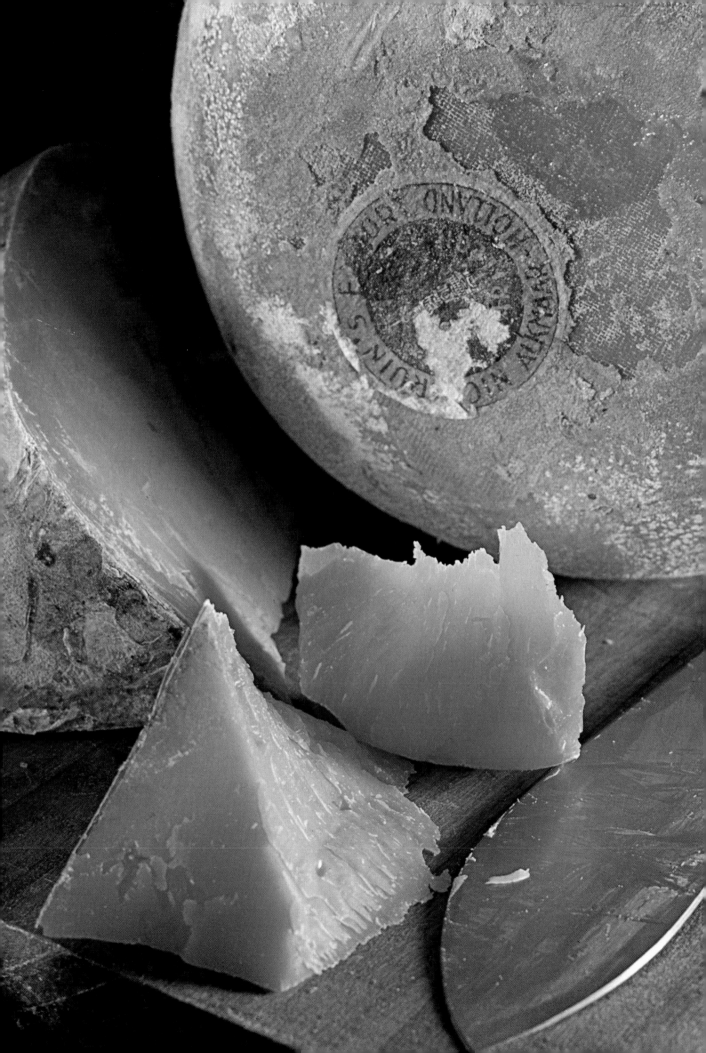

MINI FYNBO

A smaller sized version of the Danish cheese Fynbo. Mini Fynbo is made in 250 g ($\frac{1}{2}$ lb) sizes.
(See *Fynbo*.)

MITZITHRA

A Greek cheese made from the surplus whey left over when making Feta. Fresh sheep's milk is added to the whey and the two are mixed and curdled. After the whey has been removed the curd is drained and pressed and sold fresh and unripened. The cheese is also known as Pot Cheese—a type of Greek cottage cheese.

MOE

This is one of the two Camembert-style cheeses made in Australia. Moe, also known as Mountain Boy, comes from Victoria. The other Australian Camembert is Riviana from New South Wales.
(See *Camembert*.)

MOLBO

Country of origin: Denmark.

Background: Molbo is a Danish version of the Dutch cheese Edam, and was once known as Danish Edam.

Description: Molbo is a ball-shaped cheese with a small flat area top and bottom, which weighs approximately 2-3 kg (4-6 lb). The cheese has a dry, yellowish rind, red-waxed and a bright yellow to white interior. Its texture is firm and supple and contains a few regularly shaped holes—pea-sized or smaller. In flavour it is mild, bland, buttery, just slightly salty with a slightly acid aftertaste. Molbo is made from cow's milk.

Wines: Beaujolais-style reds, light dry whites.
Serve: End of meals, snacks; the cheese slices well, making it good for sandwiches; its bland-ness makes it suitable for children. Molbo goes with vegetables such as radishes, green peppers and grated carrots.
Fat content: 45 per cent (minimum).
Type: Bland/buttery.
Aroma: Unpronounced.

MONCENISIO

This is an Italian blue vein cheese similar to Gorgonzola.
(See *Gorgonzola*.)

MON CHOU

A Dutch double crème cheese with a 73 per cent fat content made in 100 g ($3\frac{1}{2}$ oz) packs wrapped in aluminium foil. Soft, very rich and creamy with a faintly acid tinge.
(See *Double Crèmes*.)

MONSEER

Country of origin: Germany.

Description: Monseer is a washed rind, monastery style cheese made from cow's milk. It has a thin, reddish-yellow rind. The cheese's interior is semi-soft, supple feeling, yellow in colour and dotted with a few irregular shaped holes. The cheeses are made in small wheel shapes about 15 cm (6 in) in diameter by 5 cm (2 in) thick; they weigh about 1 kg ($2\frac{1}{4}$ lb). Smaller versions are also marketed.

The cheese has a full, distinctive, lingering taste, earthy and appealing, sharpish but not overstrong; somewhere between Esrom and Munster. It has also been compared to a mild Limburger.

Wines: Goes with reds and also a good cheese to eat with beer.
Serve: Good snack-type cheese.
Fat content: 50 per cent.
Type: Monastery.
Aroma: Noticeable but not overpronounced.

MONSIEUR

Country of origin: France.

Background: This is a Normandy cheese developed towards the end of last century by a farmer named, appropriately enough, Fromage (cheese). Consequently it is sometimes known as Monsieur Fromage.

Description: Monsieur is a soft cheese with a bloomy rind, like Camembert and Brie, 7.5 cm (3 in) in diameter and about 5 cm (2 in) thick. It is made from cow's milk in a method similar to Brie, but is enriched with cream and has a higher fat content. The cheese has a downy white rind dotted with red pigments, a fresh, pleasant aroma and a rich, fruity, pronounced creamy flavour. It can be considered a richer, creamier, fuller Brie-style cheese. At its peak condition, it is highly regarded.

Wines: Full-bodied burgundy-style reds.
Serve: End of meals.
Fat content: 60 per cent.
Type: Matured double crème/Brie/Camembert.
Aroma: Unpronounced.

MONTASIO

A hard Italian cheese made in the Swiss style and similar to the more famous Fontina. Fully matured versions of this cheese are used for grating.
(See Fontina.)

MONTEREY JACK

Country of origin: USA.

Background: A Cheddar-style cheese originally from Monterey County, California, believed to have first been made in 1892. It is still made in California but also in other parts of America such as Wisconsin.

Description: The cheese is made in loaf and also wheel shapes. The largest size would be in the region of 18 kg (40 lb) but smaller sizes are made. There are two varieties, one made from whole cow's milk and one from skimmed milk. Monterey Jack is more white than yellow as the cheese is not treated with a colouring additive. It has a thin natural rind (it can also be obtained in rindless blocks) and a supple, resilient texture. The cheese is matured for only between three and six weeks which puts it at the very mild end of the Cheddar taste scale. One variety is aged for six months and is used for grating.

Wines: Light reds; dry whites.
Serve: As a snack; goes reasonably well with most vegetables and fruit.
Fat content: 50 per cent.
Type: Cheddar.
Aroma: Unpronounced.

MONTHERY

A Brie type French cheese made in two sizes: the larger one has a 35 cm (14 in) diameter and weighs about 2 kg (5 lb); the smaller weighs about 1¼ kg (3 lb).
(See Brie.)

MONTRACHET

Country of origin: France.

Background: This semi-fresh (it can be matured for as little as a week) goat's milk cheese from Burgundy takes its name from the famous white wine associated with the area. It is also known as Chèvre du Montrachet.

Description: Montrachet is made in 10 cm (4 in) tall cylinder shapes about 5 cm (2 in) in diameter. This is a soft, moist, pure white cheese with scarcely any discernible rind and a texture close to cottage cheese. The cheese is one of the best examples of the mild, fresh French chèvres—at its best light and delectable but still distinctively 'goaty'. It is usually packed in chestnut or grape leaves in containers; some versions are ash covered. Besides the standard log shape, it is also made in a creamier version packaged in 200 g (6 oz) plastic cups.

COURGETTE AND ITS FLOWER WITH RICOTTA

4 tbsp tomato sauce
1-2 courgettes, thinly sliced
Olive oil
250g ricotta
Sea salt and freshly ground black pepper
1-2 large courgette flowers, torn
2 tsp chopped marjoram

Shape your dough and put olive oil around the crust. Start with a tomato sauce base, add the courgettes and drizzle with olive oil, season with salt and pepper and top with blobs of ricotta and torn courgette flowers before baking. Once cooked, top with marjoram.

SAN DANIELE

4 tbsp tomato sauce
125g fior di latte (cow's milk) mozzarella, chopped
2 good handfuls of rocket
6 slices of San Daniele prosciutto
Olive oil

Shape your dough and put olive oil around the crust. Spread the tomato sauce on the base. Top with the fior di latte mozzarella and put in the oven. Finish the cooked pizza with rocket and sliced prosciutto, and drizzle over some olive oil.

TABLE TALK

AA GILL

institutionally sexist habitats, and you write about the distinction between the front and back trotters of pigs, but you never mention the one between human sexes in dining rooms." Obviously my first reaction was: there, there, shouldn't you be cutting out Lucas's recipes next door? And the second thing was that I've just used the phrase "bel canto", having no idea what it means, other than a vaguely Italian operatic term that translates as beautiful song. So I've just phoned half-a-dozen people who should know, and they've given me airily cultured definitions boiling down to "it's beautiful singing" or, alternatively, "singing beautifully". Plainly, it means whatever you like. There are any number of cultural terms that are bandied and flounced in conversations as polite swearwords, emphatic punctuation, menu adjectives, imbued with an empty gravitas as civilised ballast for a light argument (see above). So I'm kidnapping bel canto and handing her over to the rough mouths to do as they will. Make it a swearword, you fat bel canto. A word for all occasions: went out last night, got truly bel cantoed. Where does all the bel canto in your bellybutton come from? The couple in the next room were giving it bel canto. We sat and watched the sun set – it was a bel canto moment.

Back to women at table. The reason I don't write about feminism is because I'm a man – most of the time – and I really don't think it's my place. When matters of feminism come up, I generally giggle and murmur, don't ask me, speak to the Blonde. I might add, quietly, while blushing in a shyly attractive way, that if I had to choose the two things that have changed and improved the lives of men most since the end of the war, it would have to be feminism and cheap,

but it's been nothing but upside for men. If you visit any society that still boasts a two-tier social system with insecure, macho and status-conscious men, you'll see women who are wary and distant around them, but who are incredibly solid, amused and supportive of each other. Where the sexes are equal, men get twice as many friends who have opinions, aspirations, expectations about happiness and careers and sex, who tell jokes and share the load. Where is the downside in that?

If we went anywhere near feminism, we'd ruin it, like we've ruined everything else. We'd turn it into a club or a competition or rugby league rules. No, no, best to say nothing and defer to the little lady. But that's not to say I haven't noticed that restaurants still look as if they're run by a collective of the Taliban and La Cage aux Folles. There are one or two female head chefs; a handful of women work in kitchens, although they are still disproportionately shoved up the dessert and petit fours end. Mostly women serve, flattering and flirting, as waitresses, managers and door Stasi. They're asked to wear "sophisticated" uniforms and work in high heels. Apart from the brilliant example of Camellia Panjabi and her sister, who set up Masala Zone, I can't think of any large restaurant or group that is owned or has a chief executive who is a woman.

The Blonde left school and trained to be a professional chef in Paris. She came back and had an interview at Le Gavroche. She was young and keen, and a terrific cook. The old Rouxs – not the one who runs it now – took a long, hard look at her, smiled and said, you'd be wasted in the kitchen. You wouldn't like the heat. Come and work front of house, my dear. So she turned on her heel and became a model, perhaps proving them right, or just proving that, well, as I said, I don't get involved in these arguments.

The whole business of dining is still stuffed with obsolete sexual attitudes. Sit in any Friday-night-date restaurant and watch the body language. Men talking, women listening. Men calling waiters, men being presented with bottles and bills. All the arch ritual etiquette of dinner as a sexual audition. And

L'ANIMA ★★★★ FOOD ★ ATMOSPHERE
1 SNOWDEN STREET, BROADGATE WEST, LONDON EC2; 020 7422 7000
LUNCH, MON-FRI, 11.45AM-3PM; DINNER, 5.30PM-11PM, SAT, 5.30PM-11.30PM

★★★★ HEART AND SOUL   ★★★★ DOVER SOUL   ★★★★ DAVID SOUL   ★★★ SOUL DESTROYING   ★ DARK NIGHT OF THE SOUL

- Sea salt
- Sugar
- Olive oil
- A handful of black olives
- 125g burrata (mozzarella filled with cream, try natoora.co.uk)

Crush the tomatoes in your hands and then put in a sieve or clean dishcloth to remove the juice. Season the tomato pulp with thyme, salt and a little sugar, and drizzle with olive oil. Place in a roasting tin and roast for 7 minutes at 180C/Gas

Portobello mushrooms with taleggio cheese

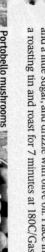

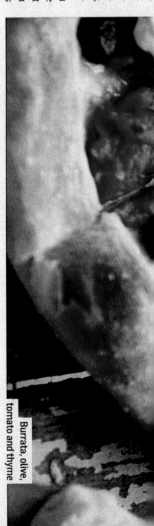

Burrata, olive, tomato and thyme

Mark 4, then allow to cool. Shape your dough and put olive oil around the crust. Place balls of the pulp around the pizza and sprinkle with olives. Bake until golden and remove from the oven, tear the burrata and place around the pizza, drizzle with olive oil and sprinkle over some more thyme.

PORTOBELLO MUSHROOMS WITH TALEGGIO CHEESE

Portobello mushrooms (2-3 per pizza, depending on size)
Sea salt and freshly ground black pepper
1 clove of garlic, finely chopped
Olive oil
4 tbsp tomato sauce
150g taleggio cheese, grated
1 tbsp oregano leaves

Clean and slice the portobello mushrooms, season with salt and pepper, place them in a baking dish and add chopped garlic and olive oil. Roast at 180C/Gas Mark 4 for 12 minutes so they are par-cooked. Allow to cool. Shape your dough and put olive oil around the crust. Put the tomato sauce on the base of the pizza, top with the mushrooms and cheese and place in the oven. Sprinkle over the oregano just before serving.

ANCHOVY, CHILLI AND CAPERS

4 tbsp tomato sauce
50g anchovies
1 red chilli, finely chopped
125g fior di latte (cow's milk) mozzarella, chopped
2 tbsp capers
2 tsp dried oregano

Shape your dough and put olive oil around the crust. Spread the tomato sauce over the base. Top with the anchovies, chopped chilli, cheese and capers. Bake in the oven until golden. Add the oregano before serving.

ST For a tasty potato and prosciutto pizza recipe, go to thesundaytimes.co.uk/style

2 Cheese descriptions

milk. A well balanced blue-veined cheese, piquant and distinctive, interesting and complex in taste—well regarded.

Wines: Full-bodied reds.
Serve: End of meals; the Norwegians recommend it on bread and butter covered with chopped radishes, topped off with canned fruit, parsley and lettuce.
Fat content: 45 per cent.
Type: Blue vein.
Aroma: Light mould smell.

NORWEGIAN EDAM

A close model of the traditional Dutch cheese. It has a slightly acid flavour but is very buttery with a sprinkling of small even holes throughout. Yellow in colour.
(See *Edam.*)

NORWEGIAN EMMENTALER

A sweeter, more watery version of the famous Swiss cheese, not so recognisably nutty in flavour.
(See *Emmentaler.*)

NORWEGIAN SAINT PAULIN

Originally modelled on the famous French cheese, this is creamy soft, pliable in texture, rather plastic, quite mild.
(See *Port Salut* and *Saint Paulin.*)

OKA

Country of origin: Canada.

Background: Oka cheese was developed by the Trappist monks at Oka in Quebec.

Description: In shape, style and size Oka is very similar to Port Salut and Saint Paulin. However, it is considered a very fine example of this style of cheese—rich, creamy, tangy and distinctive.

Wines: Full-bodied beaujolais-style wines.
Serve: End of meals.
Fat content: 45-50 per cent.
Type: Monastery.
Aroma: Unpronounced.
(See *Port Salut* and *Saint Paulin.*)

OKATO MATURED

A New Zealand Cheddar and, as the name suggests, a well matured one—a good, fulsome, strong tasting cheese.
(See *Cheddar.*)

OLIVET

This is a soft, bloomy rind cheese from the Orléans area of France. There are two kinds: Olivet Bleu which has a bluish surface mould and Olivet Cendré which is coated with and matured in ashes. Both are Camembert type cheese, Olivet Cendré being the stronger flavoured of the two. Rarely seen outside of France.
(See *Camembert.*)

OLMUTZER QUARGEL

This is a Bavarian cheese which is a member of the German family of sour curd cheeses. These cheeses are noted for their low fat content, high protein value, aroma and penetrating flavour. Olmützer Quargel is a particularly strong version of this type of cheese.
(See *Sour Curd Cheeses, Harz* and *Mainz.*)

PANEDDA

An Italian pasta filata (drawn curd) style cheese. The more famous cheeses of this type are Caciocavallo and Provolone, widely used in cooking for lasagne-type dishes.
(See *Pasta Filata* and *Provolone.*)

PANNERONE

Country of origin: Italy.

Background: This is a stracchino cheese closely related to Gorgonzola.

Description: The full name of this cheese in Italian is Stracchino di Gorgonzola bianco or Gorgonzola dolce. It is called White Gorgonzola because it is ripened for no longer than one month and does not take on the greenish-blue veining of its famous relative.

Apart from this important point the cheese is made in a similar fashion to Gorgonzola. In appearance it is flat, rectangular in shape, yellow in colour with a series of small holes set closely together. The cheeses can weigh up to about 10 kg (22 lb). Pannerone is milder than Gorgonzola, lacking the latter's pungency, but with a certain tang or middling sharpness to its taste.

Wines: Full-bodied reds.
Serve: End of meals.
Fat content: 48 per cent.
Type: Bland/buttery.
Aroma: Unpronounced.

PARMESAN

Country of origin: Italy.

Background: This is the best-known of Italy's large range of Grana cheeses, so-called because of their granular texture, which have been made in Italy since the thirteenth century. Other cheeses, which are often marketed under the name Parmesan outside Italy, include Lodigiano, Lombardo, Veneto, Bresciano, Grana Padano and Emiliano. Parmesan's correct name is Parmigiano Reggiano and it was first made in the area of Parma.

Description: Parmesan is the world's most famous grating cheese, used to complement and flavour a great variety of dishes. It is made in large cylindrical wheels up to 45 cm (18 in) in diameter and 23 cm (9 in) thick. The cheese is straw yellow in colour with a hard, brownish rind often coated with a blackish protective mixture of oil and umber.

The cheeses can spend up to three years maturing, which gives them a very hard but brittle and flaky texture making them ideal for grating. Due to its hard texture and low moisture content, the cheese will keep almost indefinitely. In flavour Parmesan is sharp, piquant and distinctive. An official Italian publication on the subject describes the cheese as having a 'fragrant, delicate taste but not spicy' and 'melting in the mouth when eaten'.

Australian Parmesan undergoes a minimum maturing period of one year but this is often extended up to two. It is made in 13 kg (29 lb) cylindrical forms and at least one company markets the cheese with the traditional waxy black surface coating. It is also available in wedges and in grated form, but all Parmesans are at their best when freshly grated.

American Parmesan is made chiefly in Wisconsin and Michigan and is matured for a minimum of fourteen months.

Wines: Full-bodied reds such as Chianti.
Serve: Parmesan's piquant flavour complements many dishes, including savoury sauces and omelettes. Mixed with fresh unripened cheeses such as Ricotta, it can be used as a filling for ravioli and cannelloni dishes. It can be sprinkled over pizzas and soups such as minestrone and used with buttered noodles, spaghetti and rice.
Fat content: 32-35 per cent.
Type: Extra-hard grating cheese.
Aroma: Unpronounced.

PASTA FILATA

The name refers not to a cheese but to a range of Italian cheeses which have their curds placed in hot water after the whey has been drained off. While the curd is in a plastic and malleable condition, it is drawn out and stretched and manipulated into shape by hand. Aged cheeses of this type can be used for grating. Examples include Caciocavallo and Provolone. Other types, such as Mozzarella and Scarmorza, are not ripened and are softer in texture and rather moist. They are often used in cooking, particularly for pizzas.
(See *Caciocavallo, Provolone, Mozzarella.*)

restricted to the use of one firm (S.A.F.R.) but numerous other firms produce Saint Paulin, a cheese very similar.

Wines: Fruity red wines.
Serve: A thoroughly satisfying snack-type cheese but also one that is likely to be enjoyed by most tastes if served at the end of a meal.
Fat content: 45-50 per cent.
Type: Monastery.
Aroma: Unpronounced.

POT CHEESE

Another name for Cottage Cheese.
(See *Cottage Cheese*.)

POULIGNY-SAINT-PIERRE

A French chèvre or goat's milk cheese made in the shape of a small pyramid.
(See *Chèvres*.)

PROCESSED CHEESE

By and large processed cheese has had a hard time at the hands of cheese writers. Variously described as the 'mongrels'[1] of the cheese world, a 'moron-like rindless child by sterilization out of tinfoil'[2] and 'solidified floor wax'[3], processed cheese has never been, and is not likely to be, placed in the gold medal class in international gourmet competitions.

Nevertheless, the humble processed cheese is enormously popular. In the USA, for example, it is estimated that one-third of the cheese made is processed. The reasons are obvious; the cheese is cheaper, it keeps well, it is easy to spread and slice, it will travel, melts easily, is nutritious and is bland to the point of innocuousness in flavour, unlikely to offend the most delicate of taste buds. This last point makes the cheese acceptable to children. Processed cheese is a good, economical, all-purpose family cheese.

[1] English food writer T. E. Layton.
[2] English wine and food expert Andre Simon.
[3] American cheese enthusiast Clifton Fadiman.

The reason that cheese buffs shudder gently at its name is that processed cheese has had its ripening process arrested at a given point by heat treatment. This means that the cheese can never develop the personality, character, individuality and flavour of natural cheese because the micro-organisms that help create these things have been effectively killed off.

Processed cheese is made by finely grinding, and mixing together by heating and stirring, one or more cheeses of the same or two or more varieties. An emulsifying agent is added and the result is a homogeneous plastic mass. Certain cheeses—Neufchâtel, Cottage, Creamed Cottage, cooked, hard grating, semi-soft, part skim, part skim spiced and skim milk cheeses —are not used. Lactic, citric, acetic or phosphoric acid or small amounts of cream, water, salt, colouring and spices or other flavouring materials may be added. The cheese may be smoked or it may be made from smoked cheese, or so-called liquid smoke flavour may be used. That description is taken practically verbatim from a US Department of Agriculture publication.

The history of processed cheese goes back to the early part of this century, being pioneered by the Swiss and eventually copied by cheese-producing countries throughout the world. Today vast amounts of processed Cheddar are manufactured, and there are also processed versions of Limburger, Gruyère, Emmentaler and the American Brick.

A marked trend has been the production of flavoured processed cheeses and cheese spreads. The following is just a sampling of some of the popular brand names and varieties sold on the world market.

AUVERNOIS (France): A processed Gruyère with either walnuts or almonds throughout as well as on the surface.

BAVARIAN (Germany): Flavoured with mushroom, pineapple, capsicum, chives, caraway, walnut, spring onion, garlic.

BAYERNLAND (Germany): Varieties flavoured with chives, mushroom, walnut, spices.

CREME CHERRY (Norway): Kirsch flavoured; another variety flavoured with walnut pieces.

A selection of mild-flavoured cheeses, predominantly processed cheeses

DANISH CHEF (Denmark): Varieties flavoured with fish, shrimp, crab, lobster, salmon, pepper, horseradish.

GOURMANDISE (France): Varieties flavoured with garlic, herb, port wine, cherry, walnut.

GRUNLAND (Germany): The trade name for a great range of processed cheeses—typical of the variety is the one studded with salami pieces particularly popular in the USA.

LAUGHING COW (France): Processed Gruyère in a large range of shapes and sizes.

RAMBOL (France): Walnut flavoured or with pieces of walnut impressed in it; there is also a peppered version.

REGAL PICON (France): Flavoured with cherry, kirsch, walnut pieces, green pepper.

SAMOS 90 (France): Spreads flavoured with mushroom, raisins, walnuts.

TIGER (Switzerland): Flavours of celery, caraway, mustard.

And so on. It is fair to say there is a flavoured processed cheese or spread available to suit almost any taste. It is also fair to say that the taste sensation you get when eating such a cheese is that of the flavouring additive. The cheese itself sits quietly in the background—mild, innocuous, rather plastic and undemanding.

PROVOLETTI

A member of the pasta filata family of Italian cheeses. Aged varieties of these cheeses are used in cooking. This cheese is essentially a small sized Provolone.
(See *Pasta Filata* and *Provolone*.)

PROVOLONE

Country of origin: Italy.

Background: Provolone, made from cow's milk, is a latter-day descendant of the Italian cheese Caciocavallo. Both are pasta filata or drawn curd cheeses. Provolone originated in southern Italy but is now made in several other countries, including America and Australia.

Description: This cheese can take a variety of shapes such as a truncated cone, a pear, a sausage or a cylinder. On its surface it often bears the marks or indentations left by the cords from which it hangs, in pairs, while maturing. Provolone, which is smoked, has a firm, smooth, shiny, golden yellow rind and a cream white interior free of holes. It is a supple-textured cheese which cuts cleanly and evenly without any flaking or crumbling. Young Provolones (those matured for between two and three months) are milder tasting than the aged variety, but still distinctive, and are used as table cheeses. The older versions (aged up to six months and longer) are often used as grating and cooking cheese. These cheeses are more granular in texture, more robust in flavour and saltier.
  As Provolone undergoes a 'cheddaring' process when it is made it is also related to the Cheddar family.
  Provolones are normally made in weights from 3.5 kg to 6 kg (8-14 lb). The pear shaped variety is the most common. Larger sized cheeses which can weigh up to 90 kg (200 lb) are known as Provolone Giganti.

Wines: Reds such as chianti.
Serve: As a table cheese Provolone goes well with bread and biscuits, pineapple wedges, dried apricots, red and green peppers and spring onions. Grated it can be used as a grilled topping to hamburgers, chicken pieces or veal or as a stuffing for ravioli, canneloni or as a melted topping to pizzas. Coated with egg and breadcrumbs and quickly pan-fried till crisp and golden brown, Provolone makes a delicious snack or appetiser.
Fat content: 45 per cent.
Type: Grating cheese/Cheddar.
Aroma: Unpronounced.

PYRAMIDE

Several French goat's milk cheeses or *chèvres* are called Pyramide because they are made in the shape of a small pyramid with the top cut off. Valençay, Levroux and Pouligny Saint Pierre are three such cheeses; some types are coated with wood ashes.

Another variety marketed as Pyramide White and Black has a thin, edible crust with a soft, ivory white interior paste. Such cheeses are generally at the mild flavoured end of the French *chèvres* range.
(See *Valençay*.)

QUARDO

Another name for the stracchino style Italian cheese, Milano.
(See *Stracchino* and *Milano*.)

QUARK

A type of fresh, unripened Cottage Cheese made in Europe. Such Continental-style Cottage Cheeses appear as a solid mass rather than as a mass of separate curd particles. Widely used in cooking.
(See *Cottage Cheese*.)

QUART

A type of Maroilles—a strong smelling, gamy and pungent tasting French washed rind cheese.
(See *Maroilles*.)

QUESO ANEJO

This is a Mexican skim-milk cheese which is matured for periods up to eight months. (The name means 'aged cheese'.) The cheese itself is dry, white and has a rather crumbly texture. In Mexico it is sometimes served with enchiladas. When covered with red chili powder it is known as Queso Enchilado.

QUESO BLANCO

This cheese is made throughout South America under a variety of names and in a variety of styles. Types are made from whole cow's milk and skimmed milk; some versions are smoked. In its many varieties the cheese can appear as a cottage cheese, cream cheese, grating cheese or a firm textured table cheese. Essentially it's the same cheese but the different manufacturing methods, maturing times, sizes and shapes result in a range of flavours and textures. The name means 'white cheese'.

RACLETTE

Country of origin: Switzerland.

Background: A cheese from the Canton of Valais and therefore often known as Valais Raclette. This cheese is used in a special toasted dish called raclette. The dish and the cheese take their name from the French *racler*—'to scrape'.

Description: Raclette is made in wheel shapes up to 9 kg (20 lb). The cheese has a light-brown natural rind with a firm textured interior, pale yellow to light brown in colour, which is scattered with holes. Like all the major Swiss cheeses Raclette is a hard, pressed cooked cheese. It is made from cow's milk and matured for up to six months.

As a table cheese Raclette is mild but distinctive, rather nut-like, palatable and tasty. It can be compared to Gruyère.

Wines: Dry white wines; can also go with beer.
Serve: As a table cheese at end of meals. When used in raclette, the cheese is placed on a heated griddle until it begins to melt, then, when sizzling, it is scooped off with a knife onto toast placed alongside the griddle. Traditionally the cheese was scraped onto boiled potatoes.

Fat content: 50 per cent.
Type: Swiss.
Aroma: Unpronounced.

RAGNIT

A cheese first produced by Dutch settlers in the region of Tilsit in east Prussia last century. It is more commonly known as Tilsit.
(See *Tilsit*.)

RAMBOL

A French processed cheese range flavoured with, and often studded with, nuts.
(See *Processed Cheese*.)

REBLOCHON

Country of origin: France.

Background: This is a centuries-old cheese from the Savoy mountain area of France. Herdsmen tending the cows would leave enough milk for a second milking on the days when the milk quotas were checked. The herdsmen would milk the cows for a second time after the inspection, keeping the results of this milking (what they considered to be the 'richest' milk) for themselves. It was from this practice that Reblochon developed and took its name. *Reblocher* means 'second milking'.

Description: Reblochon is a soft, surface-ripened, washed-rind cheese made in flat discs about 12.5 cm (5 in) in diameter and 2.5 cm (1 in) thick. It has a reddish-coloured outer rind, smooth with a matt finish, and a pale creamy interior. The cheese is matured for about four weeks.

A very attractive cheese, essentially mild tasting but creamy, yielding, vaguely nutty—held in high esteem by cheese buffs. At its best it should feel supple and plump. Past its prime it develops a bitter taste.

Wines: Light and fruity beaujolais style reds.
Serve: End of meals.
Fat content: 50 per cent.
Type: Monastery.
Aroma: Unpronounced.

RECUIT

A whey, Cottage style cheese, the best known version of which is Ricotta.
(See *Ricotta*.)

RED CHESHIRE

A Cheshire cheese treated with an annatto dye which gives it its reddish colouring—originally carrot juice was used. Cheshire comes in three varieties, red, white and blue—a very patriotic cheese.
(See *Cheshire*.)

REDSKIN

(See American *Cheddars*.)

REGAL PICON

A well-known brand name for a range of French processed cheese which can be flavoured with kirsch, walnut pieces or green peppers.
(See *Processed Cheese*.)

REMOUDOU

A Belgian cheese related to Limburger and Hervé. All three are washed rind cheeses and are noted for their pungent aromas. Both Remoudou and Hervé have a highly pronounced gamy taste.
(See *Hervé*.)

Red Cheshire (photo by Russell Cockayne)

REYBIER

Brand name for a large range of French processed cheese. Flavourings vary, but include herbs, kirsch, pepper, hazelnuts, almonds and a smoked variety.
(See *Processed Cheese*.)

RICOTTA

Country of origin: Italy.

Background: This cheese, sometimes known as 'whey' or 'albumin' cheese, is a type of Italian Cottage Cheese.

Description: Ricotta is made from the whey drained from the cheese curd when making Provolone. Although liquid, the whey still contains a protein known as lactalbumin. When heated the whey coagulates in a similar fashion to the white of an egg. Acids such as vinegar are added and often extra milk also to improve the balance, fat content and quality of the cheese. The cheese is made from cow's milk and does not undergo a ripening process. Pure white in colour, Ricotta has a fine, slightly moist texture and a bland, sweetish flavour. It comes as a smooth white mass and is packaged in a variety of shapes, sizes, tubs and containers. As with all fresh, unripened cheeses, Ricotta does not have a long life and should be used within a short time of purchase. The cheese can be cured and salted, when it becomes Dry Ricotta, used as a grating cheese.

Ricotta-style cheese is made in various parts of Europe under a variety of names such as Ziger, Sérac, Brocotte, Mejette, Schottenziger and Recuit.

American Ricotta, made chiefly in Wisconsin and New York, has between 5 and 10 per cent whole or skimmed milk added to it. The whole milk is used in fresh Ricotta which tends to be creamier and sweeter than the Italian version; skimmed milk for Dry Ricotta.

Ricotta Salata is a hard, flaky version made in a ball-shape and used in salads in a similar way to Feta.

Australian Ricotta is made in several states. The cheese is often marketed in parchment wrapped portions or in plastic containers of 500 g (1 lb).

Wines: Light whites, reds, rosés or coffee, depending on how the cheese is used.
Serve: Ricotta is well suited as a base for a variety of sweet and savoury dishes. It can be used as a dessert cheese, sprinkled with sugar and eaten with fresh fruit; as a health food lunch or a snack with dried fruits and chopped nuts intermixed and muesli added to thicken it. To make an interesting cheese dip try it with a packet of onion soup made to half strength, or with an equal portion of blue vein cheese and some fresh herbs, or with curry powder and yoghurt.
Fat content: 4-10 per cent.
Type: Whey cheese, fresh, unripened.
Aroma: Unpronounced.

RICOTTA SALATA

A hard Ricotta, very flaky, made in ball shapes weighing just over 2 kg (up to 5 lb). The cheese is used in salads in a similar fashion to Feta.
(See *Ricotta*.)

RIDDER

Country of origin: Norway.

Background: This cheese is a Norwegian version of Saint Paulin.

Description: Ridder is usually marketed in small wheel shapes some 23 cm (9 in) in diameter. The cheese has a wax rind and is pale yellow in colour. The interior paste is firm and supple-textured, dotted with small holes.

Made from cow's milk, its flavour is mild, smooth and creamy with a lightly piquant aftertaste. In texture, taste and bouquet it can be considered a creamier version (the cheese has a higher fat content) of Saint Paulin.

Wines: Burgundy-style reds.
Serve: End of meals or as a snack.
Fat content: 60 per cent.
Type: Monastery/double crème.
Aroma: Unpronounced.

RIVIANA

One of two Camembert style cheeses made in Australia. Riviana comes from New South Wales. The other Australian Camembert is Moe from Victoria.
(See *Camembert*.)

ROBIOLA

An Italian stracchino style cheese which is made in two sizes, the smaller one being the stronger tasting.
(See *Stracchino*.)

ROLLOT

A soft, washed rind cheese made in small flat cylinder shapes measuring 7.5 cm (3 in) in diameter and 2.5 cm (1 in) thick. This is quite a spicy, full flavoured French cheese with a noticeable aroma similar in some ways to Pont l'Evêque. Rollot is a cheese not usually encountered outside France.
(See *Pont l'Evêque*.)

ROMADUR

Country of origin: Germany.

Background: This cheese, which is chiefly produced in Bavaria, falls in what the Germans call the *roschmier* range—soft cheeses with a reddish tinge. These are surface-ripened, washed-rind cheeses whose surface is smeared with a mould-producing bacteria. Limburger is the best-known cheese of this type.

Description: The cheese is marketed in sizes weighing from 125 g (¼ lb) up to 500 g (1 lb). It is made in bar and square shapes, a standard size being 12.5 cm (5 in) long and 5 cm (2 in) square. Romadur is made from whole or partly skimmed cow's milk and has a smooth rind with a yellowish-brown to reddish tinge. The interior is pale yellow with a few holes.

Romadur can be compared to Limburger but it contains less salt, is ripened for a shorter period (up to five weeks) at a lower temperature and has a smaller degree of surface bacterial smear. Consequently neither the flavour nor the aroma is as pronounced as that of Limburger. All in all, a milder Limburger style cheese.

Wines: Full-bodied reds, beer.
Serve: A good snack type cheese.
Fat content: Approximately 47 per cent.
Type: Monastery.
Aroma: Noticeable, but not over-pronounced.

ROMANO

A hard Italian grating cheese which is also known as Incanestrato. When made from sheep's milk it is known as Pecorino Romano; from cow's milk Vacchino Romano and from goat's milk Caprino Romano. Sardo Romano is a version made in Sardinia. When these cheeses are cured for less than a year they are used as table cheeses.
(See *Pecorino Romano*.)

RONDELE

A range of double crème cheeses which are flavoured with pepper, garlic and herbs; an unflavoured version is also available. All are rich and creamy, with the flavouring agents providing a tang.
(See *Double Crèmes*.)

ROQUEFORT

Country of origin: France.

Background: Of all the blue-veined cheeses, this is the oldest and to many minds the best. Throughout recorded history it has certainly not lacked for notable propagandists. Pliny the Elder thought it the best cheese in Rome two thousand years ago and it was a great favourite of the Emperor Charlemagne in the eighth century. Even Casanova got in on the act, extolling its excellence and writing that it 'revived love' and 'brought to maturity a budding love'.

The cheese comes from the Causes, an area of limestone plateaux in the province of Aquitaine. It is made from unskimmed sheep's milk and matured in limestone caves.

The story goes that in times past a shepherd accidentally left a piece of sheep's milk cheese with some bread in one of the caves. When he came upon the cheese and bread some weeks later they had formed into one monstrous, coagulated, mould-covered mass—but it didn't taste bad!

Description: Roquefort has its curd treated with *Penicillium roqueforti*, which is found in rye bread, to develop its veining. The unique atmospheric conditions of the limestone caves in which the cheese ripens for between three and five months do the rest.

Roquefort is a cylindrical cheese with a thin, almost transparent crust. It is creamy white in colour and is marbled by a network of blue veining running through its body. The cheese measures approximately 17.5 cm (7 in) in diameter and 10 cm (4 in) in height.

Roquefort is a strong-tasting blue vein, very rich, pungent and salty, leaving a sharp sensation on the tongue and a lingering aftertaste. Exported cheeses are often too sharp and salty for some tastes, but many connoisseurs hold it to be the finest cheese in the world.

The cheese takes its name from Roquefort-sur-Soulzon where it is made.

Wines: Strong, rich red wines; port.
Serve: End of meals; if too salty mix a little butter into the cheese.
Fat content: 45 per cent.
Type: Blue vein/sheep's milk.
Aroma: Mould smell, noticeable but not over-pronounced.

ROSCHMIER

This is not an individual cheese but the word used to describe a range of German cheeses—soft cheeses with a reddish tinge. They are all washed rind cheeses, many of them quite sharp tasting.
(See *Romadur*.)

ROYALP

Country of origin: Switzerland.

Background: This is a relatively new cheese, made in eastern Switzerland and now being promoted as one of the 'big five' Swiss cheeses (the others are Emmentaler, Gruyère, Appenzell and Sbrinz).

Description: Royalp is made in wheel shapes measuring 25 cm (10 in) in diameter and 8 cm (3 in) deep. The cheese has a reddish-brown semi-hard natural rind and a softer interior paste peppered with small holes. Made from cow's milk, it is ripened for three months. In flavour it is mild but distinctive, with a piquancy in its aftertaste. By the time Royalp has reached its export markets it has normally become stronger tasting, rather like a more full-flavoured Gruyère.

Wines: Fruity reds, rosés, also beer.
Serve: A good table cheese which goes well with a variety of fruits and nuts, or in sandwiches; the cheese has good melting qualities and makes an excellent Welsh rarebit.
Fat content: 45 per cent.
Type: Swiss.
Aroma: Unpronounced.

SAANEN

This is a Swiss grating cheese similar to Sbrinz. Such cheeses can be matured for up to seven years. They taste like a very full, very matured Gruyère.
(See *Sbrinz*.)

SAGA

A rich, creamy double crème cheese from Denmark with a moulded surface and internal blue veining. The blue vein flavour is mild; the cheese is similar to Blue Castello in style and has a 70 per cent fat content.
(See *Blue Castello* and *Bavarian Blue*.)

Sbrinz (top), Royalp (below)

SAGE

Certain Cheddars which are spiced with sage are known by this name. Two of the best known are Vermont Sage (American) and Derby Sage (English). The cheeses have a greenish hue.
(See *Cheddar*.)

SAINT ANDRE

A French triple crème with a 75 per cent fat content. The cheese has a light bloomy white 'fluffy' rind, a rich, creamy, tangy flavour and texture and a noticeable bouquet.
(See *Triple Crèmes*.)

SAINT BENOIT

A small disc shaped French cheese about 7.5 cm (3 in) in diameter with a bloomy rind and soft, creamy paste. St Benoit belongs to the Brie/Camembert family and is made in two versions: with a 40 per cent and 60 per cent fat content. It is similar to Coulommiers.
(See *Coulommiers*.)

SAINT MARCELLIN

Country of origin: France.

Background: This cheese dates back to the fifteenth century. It was supposed to have been offered to the future King Louis XI after he had been rescued from a bear by two charcoal-burners in the Lenta Forest. Louis liked it so much that it was later served at the royal table.

Description: Saint Marcellin is a small, disc-shaped cheese no more than 7.5 cm (3 in) in diameter and 2.5 cm (1 in) thick. It is a soft cheese with a light natural rind or crust on which a blue-greyish mould has been cultivated. The cheese's soft interior paste is not

affected by the mould so it is not classed as a blue vein. Saint Marcellin is mild tasting but tangy with a pleasantly creamy, vaguely 'goaty' flavour. It is ripened for about one month before marketing when it often appears wrapped in chestnut leaves. The cheese was originally produced on farms and made from goat's milk but is now commercially manufactured from cow's milk.

Wines: Light and fruity reds.
Serve: End of meals.
Fat content: 50 per cent.
Type: Bland/buttery.
Aroma: Unpronounced.

SAINT MAURE

Country of origin: France.

Description: This is a French goat's milk cheese made in small cylinder shapes about 15 cm (6 in) long and 2.5 cm (1 in) in diameter. Those produced on farms have a bluish rind while the commercially made varieties have a white bloomy rind. Such cheeses are ripened for one month and have a soft creamy texture and a full, fresh 'goaty' flavour to them. Older cheeses develop a very ripe odour and flavour.

Wines: Fruity reds and whites.
Serve: End of meals.
Fat content: 45 per cent.
Type: Goat's milk.
Aroma: Lightly 'goaty'; aged cheeses are quite pungent.

SAINT NECTAIRE

Country of origin: France.

Background: This is a highly rated cheese which is made in the Auvergne province of France and is believed to date back to the Middle Ages.

Description: Saint Nectaire is made from cow's milk in flat disc shapes measuring 20 cm (8 in) in diameter and 3 cm (1½ in) thick. The

yellowish in colour with a firm but supple texture.

The cheese can be eaten fresh when its taste is mild with a delicate sweetish, nutty flavour. Older cheeses, which are sharper tasting, are used for cooking.

Wines: Light fruity reds; dry whites such as white hermitage.
Serve: Young Scarmorzas can be used as table cheeses, as snacks, or at the end of a meal; the more matured versions (those aged for between 4-6 weeks) are used as cooking cheeses, particularly in pizzas.
Fat content: 45 per cent.
Type: Fresh, unripened.
Aroma: Unpronounced.
(See *Pasta Filata*.)

SCHABZIGER

A German version of the Swiss grating cheese Sapsago, notable for the fact that it is light green in colour.
(See *Sapsago*.)

SCHMIERKASE

(See *Cottage Cheese*.)

SCHNITTKASE

The name, which means 'sliceable' cheese, is given to a group of cheeses produced in Germany which are considered suitable for slicing. They are all based on cheeses developed in other countries, apart from Tilsit, which was first produced in East Prussia. In fact, Tilsit has Dutch antecedents, having been created by immigrants from the Netherlands.

The Schnittkäse group comprises German Edam, Geheimratskäse (a smaller sized Edam), Trappist (similar to Port Salut), Tilsit (a stronger Port Salut style) and German Gouda.

SCHOTTENZIGER

A whey, Cottage style cheese, the best known version of which is Ricotta.
(See *Ricotta*.)

SCHWEIZER

This Swiss cheese is made in the shape of a small loaf and is one of the stronger tasting Gruyère type cheeses. It has an immediate flavour that dominates the palate at first bite —strong and intense.
(See *Gruyère*.)

SELLES-SUR-CHER

A young French goat's milk cheese with a charcoal powdered natural rind. The cheese is ripened for a three week period and is soft textured and mild with a noticeably nutty flavour. It is made in small 150 g (5 oz) ball shapes.
(See *Chèvres*.)

SEPTMONCEL

A French blue vein also known as Gex or Bleu du Haut Jura.
(See *Bleu du Haut Jura*.)

SERAC

A whey, Cottage style cheese, the best known version of which is Ricotta.
(See *Ricotta*.)

SERRA DA ESTRELLA

Country of origin: Portugal.

Background: This cheese is considered the best of a range of Portuguese mountain cheeses. All Serra cheeses are mountain cheeses; many

carry in addition the name of the district or mountain range in which they are made—as with Serra da Estrella.

Description: The cheese is made in thick disc shapes up to 30 cm (10 in) in diameter and 5 cm (2 in) thick. It has a compact, semi-firm texture and its cream-white interior paste is dotted with a few small holes.

The cheese is made from sheep's milk but can be made from a mixture of sheep's and goat's milk; occasionally it is made from cow's milk. One of the interesting features of this cheese is that no animal rennet is used to coagulate the milk—this is effected by an extract from a certain type of thistle.

One of the best of the European sheep's milk cheeses, Serra da Estrella is comparable to the highly rated Spanish cheese Manchego. Ripened for only a two to three week period, the cheese is essentially mild tasting yet distinctively 'sheepy', faintly piquant, oily and attractive.

Wines: Dry reds.
Serve: Snacks; an arresting and distinctive cheese for a cheese board.
Fat content: 40 per cent.
Type: Sheep's milk.
Aroma: Unpronounced.

SLIPCOTE

An English version of Cream Cheese popular in Shakespeare's time.
(See *Cream Cheese.*)

SMOKED CHEESE

Smoked cheese is not a type, but simply a variety, often Cheddar or Emmentaler, which has been flavoured by smoke. In many cases the smoke flavouring is artificially created by chemicals rather than the cheese being naturally smoked over a fire. The traditional shape of smoked cheese is that of a long sausage.

Much of the smoked cheese on the market today is processed, with flavours ranging from mild to sharpish. They are often spiced with herbs such as caraway, and other additives.

SORBAIS

A version of Maroilles, a strong smelling and pungent tasting French washed rind cheese. (See *Maroilles.*)

SOUR CURD CHEESE

Country of origin: Germany.

Background: As the name implies, these are a range of German cheeses made from the curd of skimmed sour milk. Such cheeses have the virtue of a high protein content coupled with a low fat content. Their lack of virtue for many people is that they are often extremely pronounced in taste and smell. Although the numerous varieties range in flavour from mild to extremely sharp, they are all somewhat an acquired taste.

This type of cheese has been made in Germany for more than two hundred years and the Germans take to them with great gusto, eating them with and in beer, sometimes with cider, using them to complement such delicacies as goose-dripping on bread and sometimes covering them with a mixture of vinegar-oil dressing, onions and paprika.

Description: The two best-known sour curd cheeses are Harz and Mainz. They are small, disc shaped, rubbery-textured cheeses with smooth, golden yellow to reddish-brown surfaces and pale glassy yellow interiors.

Other types are Stängen (bar), Hand (hand), Bauerhand (peasant hand), Korb (basket), Spitz (pointed) and Olmützer Quargel. (Quargel is a general name for sour curd cheeses.) Most of these are round and flat, sometimes covered with an edible mould. Spitz is flavoured with caraway seeds. Olmützer Quargel, noted for its sharpness, comes from Bavaria.

Kochkäse (cooked cheese) is produced by heating pre-ripened curd. It is mostly sold in tins or plastic containers. The cheese is very pure tasting and spreads easily.

Wines: This type of cheese goes best with beer, sometimes cider.
Serve: As a snack.

A selection of Smoked Cheeses

Fat content: Less than 10 per cent.
Type: Strong smelling.
Aroma: Pronounced.
(See *Harz* and *Mainz*.)

SOUTHBROOK CHESHIRE

Origin: Australia.

Background: A Cheshire style cheese made since 1964, in the town of Southbrook, Queensland, a few kilometres south-west of Toowoomba. This is the only Cheshire type cheese now manufactured in Australia.

Description: A crumbly textured cheese with a slight acidic tang that develops to a pronounced bite as the cheese matures. Its pale cream colour results from the high acidity of the manufacturing process. Maturing takes up to three months before sealing in 250 g ($\frac{1}{2}$ lb), 500 g (1 lb) and 2.5 kg ($5\frac{1}{2}$ lb) plastic packs.

Wines: Rich burgundies, claret; the milder flavour of a lightly matured Southbrook Cheshire suits a rosé or riesling. For cooking, it can be used as a substitute for matured natural Cheddar.
Serve: End of meals with dried apricots, figs and grapes.
Fat content: 48 per cent.
Type: Cheddar.
Aroma: Unpronounced.

SPALEN

This is a younger version of the Swiss grating cheese Sbrinz. Spalens are so called because of the wooden containers that are used to transport them. Unlike Sbrinz, they are not used for grating, but as table cheeses.
(See *Sbrinz*.)

SPICED CHEESE

Spiced cheeses cover a large range of flavours and types. Notable ones include: Lancashire Sage, a Cheddar-style cheese flavoured with sage (its American equivalent is Vermont Sage); the Dutch cheese Leyden flavoured with cumin and caraway seeds; and Friesian spiced with cloves (as is the Norwegian cheese Nokkelost). The Swiss grating cheese Sapsago has had clover added to it while the English have taken to flavouring several of their traditional cheeses with wine, cider, beer and chives. Boursin is a spiced triple crème while there is a host of processed cheeses flavoured or spiced with additives ranging from salmon to pineapple.

SPICED GOUDA

A variety of the Dutch cheese Gouda spiced with cumin seed.
(See *Gouda*.)

SPITZ

This is a member of the range of German sour curd cheeses noted for their low fat content, high protein value, full aroma and penetrating flavour. Spitz is a variety spiced with caraway seed.
(See *Sour Curd Cheeses*, *Harz* and *Mainz*.)

STANGEN

One of the range of German sour curd cheeses. The name means 'bar cheese'. These cheeses are small, rubbery textured, with smooth, golden yellow to reddish brown surfaces and pale glassy yellow interiors. They can be extremely pronounced in both taste and aroma; even mild varieties are quite distinctive and all are something of an acquired taste.
(See *Sour Curd Cheeses*, *Harz* and *Mainz*.)

STEINBUSCHER

Country of origin: Germany.

Background: This is a cheese first produced in northern Germany last century. It takes its

TUXFORD & TEBB

STILTON CHEESE

EST. 1780

CERTIFICATION TRADE MARK

ENGLISH
BLUE STILTON CHEESE

Made at
MELTON MOWBRAY
LEICESTERSHIRE
ENGLAND

name from the town where it was first developed.

Description: Steinbüscher is a cheese of the same style as Limburger, although not so full-flavoured or spicy in aroma. It is made in squares varying in weight from 200 g to 1 kg (7 oz-2¼ lb). The cheese has a reddish-brown outer rind covered with a layer of white mould, and a straw yellow interior with few holes.

The Germans place this cheese in their semi-soft, sliceable range of cheeses, which include Wilstermarsch, Edelpilz, Butter Cheese or Damenkäse and Weisslacker. Steinbüscher has a rich, buttery consistency and is at the bland end of the range—a mild-tasting German cheese only lightly piquant in taste.

Wines: Light dry whites, light reds.
Serve: End of meals, snacks.
Fat content: 50 per cent.
Type: Monastery/mild.
Aroma: Unpronounced.

STILTON

Country of origin: Great Britain (England).

Background: The 'king' of cheeses in the opinion of many experts, Stilton was first sold over two hundred years ago to coach passengers who stopped at the Bell Inn in Stilton Village in Huntingdonshire. Now recognised as one of the greatest cheeses in the world, Stilton has the distinction of being the only English cheese with a trade copyright. Stiltons are only made in parts of Leicestershire, Derbyshire and Nottinghamshire.

Description: Stilton is a blue-vein cheese, semi-firm, made from the best cream and milk. Creamy white in colour, it matures in three to six months. Immature Stiltons do not take on the network of blue veins which is created in the cheese by injection of a *Penicillium* spore. These immature cheeses are known as White Stiltons.

The cheese is made from cow's milk enriched with cream, in the shape of a tall cylinder some 15 cm (6 in) in diameter and 25 cm (10 in) high. It has a brown-greyish rind, slightly wrinkled from surface bacterial activity. The internal blue veining is dense and evenly distributed, a sign of quality in any blue vein cheese.

In flavour Stilton is distinctively piquant but rich and mellow with clean Cheddar undertones. It is not as salty as the French Roquefort and is less creamy than Gorgonzola.

To appreciate it at its best, you must look after it well. The Stilton Manufacturers' Association states that the cheese should be kept at room temperature, covered with a cloth. A cheese that has gone dry should be covered with a cloth dampened with brine (a handful of common salt in a basin of water). Stiltons can be kept in a refrigerator but for best results keep them wrapped in a damp cloth.

A widespread fallacy is that Stilton is improved by mixing port wine into it. This is a practice which dates back to Victorian times. It spoils the cheese while adding nothing to the rich succulence of the Stilton flavour. The Stilton Manufacturers' Association maintains that if the cheese is good it does not require port, and if it is a bad cheese, no amount of port is going to improve its flavour.

Wines: Port or any full-bodied burgundy.
Serve: End of meals.
Fat content: 55 per cent.
Type: Blue vein.
Aroma: Noticeable mould smell.

STRACCHINO

Stracchino is a generic name for a range of Italian cheeses, usually rich, soft, white cheese, virtually rindless, designed to be eaten fresh. Cheeses of this sort have been made since the twelfth century.

The name is derived from the word *stracca* (dialect for 'tired') and referred to the condition of cows making the long trek south over the Lombardy Plains before winter. The fact that the cows were fatigued affected the quality of their milk. Although the same situation does not exist today, the name stracchino lives on.

There are two types of stracchino—*piccante* (sharp) and *dolce* (mild). Most stracchino cheeses are ripened for short periods of ten to fifteen days and are so fresh and delicate that they rarely leave Italy.

Gorgonzola (a *piccante* type) and Taleggio are two exceptions, but both are ripened for a longer period. To add to the confusion, Stracchino is the name of a specific cheese as well as the generic name for a range.

Cheeses of this type include Crescenza (very rich, and so soft and creamy that it can be spread like butter) and Robiola (made in two sizes, the smaller being sharp-tasting). The actual cheese known as Stracchino is of the *dolce* variety—white, moist, with a plastic consistency to its texture, milky with a light tang.

SUPREME DES DUCS

A double crème produced in Neufchâtel-en-Bray. More commonly known as Suprême, the cheese is made in a small thick disc shape with a natural bloomy rind. It is ripened for two weeks. It has a 72 per cent fat content, and is voluptuously rich, soft and creamy.
(See *Double Crèmes.*)

SVECIAOST

Country of origin: Sweden.

Background: The Swedes originally created this cheese as a version of Gouda, but it has developed a character of its own.

Description: Made from cow's milk (sometimes skimmed) Sveciaost is made in wheel shapes weighing 11 kg to 13 kg (25-30 lb). The cheese has a smooth, waxed rind with a white interior scattered with small, irregularly shaped holes. In texture the cheese is firm, elastic, supple.

Numerous types of this cheese are made throughout Sweden. Fat content can vary between 30 and 60 per cent; it can be ripened for six weeks or left to mature for as long as a year; some versions are spiced with caraway seeds or a combination of caraway seeds and cloves; some are unflavoured.

All these factors affect its taste; essentially an uncomplicated, mild, bland, buttery Gouda-like cheese when young. Aged versions gain considerably in depth of taste and strength and can be quite pungent; spiced Sveciaosts are tangy and aromatic.

Wines: Simple dry reds and whites; beer.
Serve: A good snack-type cheese.
Fat content: 30-60 per cent.
Type: Bland/buttery.
Aroma: Unpronounced.

SWEET MUENSTER

A processed cheese more commonly known as Mun-Chee. The cheese is made in loaf shapes and is soft, sweet and simple—it has nothing in common with the notable French cheese, Münster.

SWEDISH FONTINA

A copy of the famous Italian cheese—rather more full flavoured than the original.
(See *Fontina.*)

TAFFEL

Country of origin: Denmark.

Background: The word *taffel* means 'table'; the cheese is a member of the Danish family of Samsoe table cheeses. The Danes now call the cheese Tybo but versions of Taffel cheese are made in several other countries.

Description: The cheese can be made in rectangular or loaf shapes in weights varying from 1.5-2.5 kg (3-6 lb). A standard size measures 19 cm by 12 cm by 12 cm (8 x 5 x 5 in). Taffel has a dry and yellowish rind often covered with a red or yellow wax. Its interior is pure yellow to white, smooth and close in texture with a few small holes and a supple, resilient body. The flavour is mild, bland and buttery.

Wines: Light whites and reds.
Serve: A good all-purpose table cheese whose slicing qualities make it ideal for sandwiches and snacks; it goes well with fruit and its mildness makes it appealing to children.
Fat content: 40-45 per cent.
Type: Bland/buttery.
Aroma: Unpronounced.

TALEGGIO

Country of origin: Italy.

Background: Taleggio is a stracchino style cheese of the *dolce* (mild) category which can be compared to Bel Paese. It comes from the Taleggio Valley in Lombardy.

Description: The cheese is pressed, uncooked, surface-ripened, and made in the shape of a 20 cm (8 in) square block 5 cm (2 in) thick. Its outer rind is rough, uneven and rosy-pink in colour; the interior varies from creamy-white to light yellow. Taleggio is semi-soft but supple and springy-feeling to the touch. It is mild but rich in flavour, full and creamy. The cheese is made from cow's milk and is ripened for about two months, the flavour growing sharper with age.

Wines: Light but lively reds and whites.
Serve: A delicious, rich, creamy cheese to serve at the end of meals with fruit.
Fat content: 48 per cent.
Type: Bland/buttery.
Aroma: Unpronounced.
(See *Stracchino*.)

TELEMES

Country of origin: Greece.

Background: This cheese is produced in several Balkan countries and is similar to Feta.

Description: Telemes is made from sheep's milk (and sometimes goat's milk) in 7.5 to 10 cm (3-4 in) squares about 5 cm (2 in) thick. The cheese is soft, moist, and creamy white in colour, and is ripened for ten days in a salt bath. Like Feta it is often called a 'pickled' cheese and is very sharp and salty to the taste.

Wines: Retsina, ouzo.
Serve: Suited for savouries, hors d'oeuvres and on cheese platters complementing dark rye breads and stuffed olives; can also be used lightly crumbled into salads.
Fat content: 40 per cent.
Type: Sheep's milk/pickled.
Aroma: Unpronounced but has a salty note.

TETE DE MOINE

This cheese is also known as Bellelaye. It is a Swiss cheese which dates back to the fifteenth century. At the monastery of Bellelaye, where the cheese originated, it was the practice for each monk to receive one cheese (per head)—hence its name. Tête de Moine resembles a more strongly flavoured Gruyère.
(See *Bellelaye*.)

TEXAS LONGHORN

(See American *Cheddars*.)

THURGAUER

A Swiss cheese similar to Royalp but with a richer, sweeter flavour.
(See *Royalp*.)

TIGER

Brand name for a Swiss range of processed cheese.
(See *Processed Cheese*.)

TILLAMOOK

An American Cheddar from Oregon—tangy and full flavoured.
(See American *Cheddars*.)

TILSIT

Country of origin: Germany.

Background: This cheese was first produced by Dutch settlers in the region of Tilsit, East Prussia, in the middle of last century. It is also known as Ragnit and is made in several other countries apart from Germany.

Description: Tilsit is made in small wheel shapes or rectangular loaves. The round variety usually measures 25 cm (10 in) in diameter and 12.5 cm (5 in) thick. In colour the cheese varies from ivory to pale yellow, with a slightly darker rind (there is also a rindless variety).

The Germans place Tilsit in their sliceable (schnittkäse) cheese category. It has a supple, resilient texture and contains numerous small holes the size of barley grains.

With their love of strong tasting cheese, the Germans sometimes make pungent, full-bodied versions of Tilsit, but often the cheese is tangy, piquant and mildly sour, somewhere between a mild Limburger and a strong Port Salut.

Tilsit is made from cow's milk, a surface-ripened cheese which is cured for between four and six months. One variety made from skim milk is flavoured with caraway seeds to give it a spicier, sharper, more pronounced flavour.

The cheese is wrapped in tinfoil or parchment before marketing.

Norwegian Tilsit is medium to sharp tasting with a rather strong aroma and a drier texture.

Wines: Liebfraumilch and spätlese style whites; reds; tawny port.
Serve: End of meals; its easy slicing qualities make it suitable for sandwiches.
Fat content: 45 per cent.
Type: Monastery.
Aroma: Varies, with age—can be noticeably pungent.

TOMMES

The word tomme simply means 'cheese' and prefixes the names of many cheeses produced in the Savoy Mountains of France.

The best known of the tommes is Tomme de Savoie, a cheese made in a cylindrical shape of 20 cm (8 in) diameter and up to 12.5 cm (5 in) thick. The cheese has a natural greyish rind dotted with reddish pigmentation and a supple-textured yellow-white interior. In taste the cheese is mildly tangy with the attractive earthy quality found in many monastery-style cheeses. The cheese is ripened for two months and is made from cow's milk. When made from goat's milk it is known as Tomme de Chèvres.

Tomme au Marc is an unusual and striking-looking variety which is partly ripened in, and covered with, a mixture of grape pulp, skins and pips. This cheese has a sharp, pronounced taste and a full, alcoholic aroma.

Other cheeses of the tommes family include Tomme au Fenouil, Tomme du Revard and Tomme Boudane. The majority of these cheeses are unlikely to be seen outside France.

TOMMES DES NEIGES

This cheese, which comes from the French Alps, is one of numerous mountain cheeses known as 'tommes' or sometimes 'tomes' (this is simply a dialect word for 'cheese'). This particular tomme derives the second part of its name from its rind which is snow white. The interior is ivory colour, semi-soft and dotted with tiny eyes. Although not overstrong in flavour, the cheese has a distinctive tang and attractive earthy quality.
(See *Tommes*.)

TOMMES DES PYRENEES

A French mountain cheese similar in texture and taste to Doux de Montagne, both related

Selection of Danish cheeses, members of the Samsoe family (from top, left to right) Samsoe, Tybo, Maribo, Molbo, Fynbo, Mini Fynbo, Baby Fynbo (photo by Russell Cockayne)

to Chilberta. Tommes des Pyrenees is milder—a semi-soft cheese with a black wax rind.
(See *Chilberta.*)

TOMME DU POITOU

A cheese from the Poitou region of France made from an equal mixture of goat's and cow's milk. The cheese is about 20 cm (8 in) in diameter and has a white downy rind. A semi-soft cheese, not as sharp as regular goat's milk cheeses.
(See *Chèvres.*)

TRAPPIST

Trappist is a general term for a monastery style cheese originated by Trappist monks. According to some authorities it is also the name of a cheese first produced in Bosnia in 1885. Cheese of this style is now made in several European countries including Hungary, Czechoslovakia and Germany.

All these cheeses are similar in style to Port Salut and Saint Paulin. The Canadian version is Oka.
(See *Port Salut*, *Saint Paulin* and *Oka.*)

TRECCIA

Background: Treccia is similar to Mozzarella, but is made in a plaited shape. It belongs to the *pasta filata* or drawn curd family of Italian cheeses.

Description: Treccia is a soft, moist white cheese with a plastic body and a smooth, close texture. Made in a plaited shape, the cheese weighs between 250 g and 500 g ($\frac{1}{2}$-1 lb) and undergoes a ripening period of only two to three days. The cheese has little aroma and a mild creamy flavour, rather delicate. It is made from cow's milk.

Wines: Light whites and reds.
Serve: Chiefly used in cooking: when heated the cheese forms long elastic strands, making it ideal for pizzas.

Fat content: 40-45 per cent.
Type: Fresh, unripened.
Aroma: Unpronounced.

TRIPLE CREMES

Country of origin: France.

Background: This type of cheese, now produced all over Europe, is a step up from the double crème type. The French define a triple crème as one which contains 75 per cent *matière grasse*, which means that butterfat accounts for 75 grams out of every 100 grams of cheese. Such information is always detailed on the cheese's packaging. Most cheeses have an average 45 per cent fat content. Consequently, triple cremes are the richest and the creamiest of cheeses. They are also relative newcomers, having first appeared in the 1950s.

Description: Triple cremes are usually made in small cylinder shapes about 7.5 cm (3 in) in diameter and 5 cm (2 in) thick. Other shapes include squares and wheels. These cheeses are made from cow's milk enriched with cream, and are usually ripened for about three weeks, when they develop a light bloomy mould on their surfaces, sometimes pigmented. They are usually creamy white in colour. Some varieties such as Fontainebleau are unripened.

As mentioned earlier, in taste and texture triple cremes are the richest, softest and creamiest cheeses of all, sometimes having a sourish piquant tinge—uncomplicated but voluptuous and delicious.

Triple cremes are sold under different brand names such as Bellétoile, Boursault, Brillat-Savarin, Lucullus, Explorateur, Magnum and Saint André.

Wines: Light spätlese-style whites; rosés; they also go with coffee.
Serve: A good choice instead of a dessert at the end of a meal; as a luxurious and totally self-indulgent snack with wafers of crisp apple or pear, or simply with cracker biscuits.
Fat content: 75 per cent.
Type: Triple crème.
Aroma: Unpronounced.

Bellétoile (left), a Triple Crème Cheese, and Rondelé, a Double Crème

TROPEFYNBO

A version of the Danish cheese Fynbo made with a thicker rind designed to enable it to withstand high temperatures.
(See *Fynbo*.)

TWIN FLATS

(See American *Cheddars*.)

TYBO

Country of origin: Denmark.

Background: Another member of the Danish family of Samsoe cheeses. It was once called Taffel.

Description: Tybo is a rectangular, loaf-shaped cheese measuring 19 cm by 12 cm by 12 cm (8 x 5 x 5 in) It has a dry, yellowish rind which may be covered with red or yellow wax. Its texture is firm and supple with a limited number of regularly shaped, pea-sized holes. Its colour is pure yellow to white and like all members of the Samsoe family it is eminently suitable for slicing. Tybo is a mild-tasting cheese, bland and buttery in consistency.

Wines: Light reds or whites; beer.
Serve: An all-purpose table cheese; its mildness makes it suitable for children.
Fat content: 45 per cent.
Type: Bland/buttery.
Aroma: Unpronounced.

UNITY BLUE

Country of origin: Australia.

Background: This Queensland cheese is the only remaining blue vein variety in Australia. Production of Unity Blue began in 1960, and is still a thriving concern. It is made at Toowoomba, Queensland.

Description: Unity Blue has a pale creamy body with a fairly open cracked texture and a generous veining of blue-green mould creating its rich piquant flavour. It is distributed throughout the eastern states of Australia in 2 kg (4½ lb) wheels and 125 g (¼ lb) foil wrapped wedges. The cheese is aged for approximately four months. To the taste it is quite sharp and tangy.

Wines: Fruity reds.
Serve: Unity Blue is complemented by dried apricots, muskatels or crisp salad vegetables. It can be easily crumbled into quiches, hot breads, salad or vegetable dressings and savoury butters.
Fat content: 48-50 per cent.
Type: Blue vein.
Aroma: Mould smell.

VACCHINO ROMANO

This Italian cheese is related to Pecorino Romano but instead of being made from sheep's milk, it is made from cow's milk. Primarily used as a hard, grating cheese.
(See *Pecorino Romano*.)

VACHERIN FRIBOURGEOIS

Country of origin: Switzerland.

Background: This is a mountain cheese of ancient origins. It is thought most likely that it is a predecessor of Gruyère and Emmentaler developed before the cheesemakers had perfected the art of 'cooking' the cheese curd.

Description: The cheese is made in the shape of a small wheel 40 cm (16 in) in diameter and 7.5 cm (3 in) thick. Vacherin Fribourgeois is made from cow's milk and has a thin, washed and brushed rind which can vary in colour from yellowish to pinkish. It is a pleasant tasting cheese which can be considered a milder, whiter type of Gruyère, lacking that cheese's complexity but palatable and faintly aromatic.

It should be noted that there are several other Vacherin cheeses made both in Switzerland and in the Savoy mountain area of

France. These include Vacherin d'Abondance, Vacherin des Aillons and Vacherin des Beauges. Vacherin Mont d'Or, a variety widely seen overseas, has a moist, pinkish rind and an interior paste so soft it is almost liquid. These cheeses are often so runny they can be eaten with a spoon.

Wines: Any light and fruity wine.
Serve: End of meals; also used in fondues.
Fat content: 45 per cent.
Type: Monastery.
Aroma: Unpronounced.

VACHERIN MONT D'OR

A Swiss mountain cheese that is made in flat cylinder shapes about 30 cm (12 in) thick. The cheese has a thin, pinkish rind and an interior so soft as to be almost liquid. Such cheeses are often so runny they can be eaten with a spoon. A mild flavoured cheese, faintly aromatic and creamy. To fully enjoy a runny Vacherin, the cheese should not be sliced. The rind should be removed and then the cheese eaten with a spoon. The French make a version of this cheese bearing the same name. These cheeses are members of the Vacherin cheese family produced in mountain areas by both the French and the Swiss.
(See *Vacherin Fribourgeois*.)

VALAIS RACLETTE

A Swiss cheese whose name is synonymous with a special toasted dish. The cheese is more commonly known as Raclette.
(See *Raclette*.)

VALEMBERT

A part skimmed cow's milk cheese made in Camembert style with a white bloomy rind. The cheese does not run as Camembert does when cut, it is not as rich and creamy, but it has a mild Camembert flavour to it—not as exciting as the true Camembert but a cheese that gives the feeling of this style of cheese while having the bonus of a low fat content. (See *Camembert*.)

VALENCAY

Country of origin: France.

Background: A goat's milk cheese from the Berry region of France, made in the shape of a small pyramid with the top cut off. Because of its shape it is sometimes known as Pyramide.

Description: Valençay is a soft, bloomy rind cheese about 7.5 cm (3 in) high and 7.5 cm by 7.5 cm (3 x 3 in) at its base. The cheese is cured for up to one month when it develops a fine downy white rind. Some varieties are coated with wood ash, which gives a bluish colour to the rind.
    Valençay is quite mild-tasting with a lightly 'goatish' aroma and flavour to it; aged cheeses are considerably more pungent.
    Other goat's milk cheeses made in a similar pyramid shape are Levroux and Pouligny Saint Pierre.

Wines: Fruity red and white wines.
Serve: End of meals to add balance to a cheese board.
Fat content: 45 per cent.
Type: Goat's milk.
Aroma: Noticeable but not over-pronounced.

VENETO

One of the lesser known of the Italian Grana style cheeses. These are cheeses that can be matured for two to three year periods. They develop very hard, brittle textures and are predominantly used in cooking as grating cheeses. The most famous is Parmesan.
(See *Grana* and *Parmesan*).

VENEZZA

An Italian grating cheese belonging to the Grana family of cheeses, the most famous of which is Parmesan.
(See *Grana* and *Parmesan*.)

VERMONT

A highly rated American Cheddar; a variety is Vermont Sage, spiced with sage flavouring. (See American *Cheddars*.)

VIEUX PANE

A large sized Pont l'Evêque which is made in a 35 cm (14 in) square, 2.5 cm (1 in) thick. Because of its size it does not dry out as quickly as the smaller Pont l'Evêque—a good point to remember when you're dealing with an imported cheese as temperamental as Pont l'Evêque. While it is rated as one of the top four French cheeses it is difficult to get in the peak of its condition outside France. Too often it dries out and develops a bitter, mouldy taste. (See *Pont l'Evêque*.)

WARSAWSKI

A Polish sheep's milk cheese similar to Kashkaval and Kasseri. An American version of Warsawski is made which is less strong and more 'Cheddary' in taste than the original Polish cheese.
(See *Kashkaval* and *Kasseri*.)

WEISSLACKER

Country of origin: Germany.

Background: This very spicy and potent little cheese is a speciality of Bavaria and is typical of the strong-smelling, sharp-tasting range of traditional German cheeses. It can be compared to Limburger.

Description: This cheese is made from a combination of skimmed and whole cow's milk and usually comes in 10 cm to 12.5 cm (4-5 in) squares about 8.75 cm (3½ in) thick. The cheese looks like a white cube of paste with virtually no rind, very few holes and a smeary, glistening surface.

Weisslacker is salted and matured for a total period of seven months, in an atmosphere of high humidity. This results in a cheese with quite some punch in taste and odour—it is something of an acquired taste, being very pungent and sharply pronounced in flavour and smell.

It is sometimes known as Bierkäse.

Wine: Does not go with wine but the Germans eat them with relish with beer; sometimes *in* their beer.
Serve: As a snack with beer.
Fat content: 40 per cent.
Type: Strong smelling.
Aroma: Pronounced.

WENSLEYDALE

Country of origin: Great Britain (England).

Background: Another very old English cheese from the Ure Valley area in Yorkshire. Its recipe is said to have been brought to England by Cistercian monks who came after the Norman Conquest in 1066. The recipe fell into the hands of local farmers' wives when the monks fled after Henry VIII ravaged Jervaulx Abbey in the sixteenth century.

Description: There are two types of Wensleydale—a white and a blue. The white takes only three weeks to mature, is clean, mild and just slightly salty to the taste, is attractively crumbly and noted for its delicious honeyed aftertaste. This last point accounts for White Wensleydale going extremely well with apple pie—a favourite combination in the north of England.
Blue Wensleydale is hard to come by nowadays, although it used to be plentiful before World War II. It is a richer, more full-bodied cheese than the white, like most good blues taking six months to mature. Rich, creamy, both tangy and sweet, it is considered by cheese buffs to be a rival to Stilton.

Wines: White Wensleydale with a light burgundy; serve the Blue with a light port or rosé.
Serve: Try the White with apple pie as a dessert; end of meals for the Blue.

Wensleydale (top and centre), Caerphilly (below)

Fat content: 45 per cent.
Type: Cheddar family/blue vein.
Aroma: The White, unpronounced; Blue Wensleydale has a tangy aroma.

WHITE GORGONZOLA

A stracchino cheese—a Gorgonzola which does not take on the greenish-blue veining of the famous Italian cheese. It is also known as Pannerone.
(See *Pannerone* and *Stracchino*.)

WHITE STILTON

A Stilton cheese which does not develop the network of veining that would make the cheese a blue vein.
(See *Stilton*.)

WILSTERMARSCH

Country of origin: Germany.

Background: The Germans place this cheese in a semi-soft category of sliceable cheeses that includes Steinbüscher, Edelpilz, Butter Cheese and Weisslacker. Wilstermarsch comes from the Schleswig-Holstein region near the Danish border. It can be considered a variety of Tilsit.

Description: The cheese, made from cow's milk, is usually produced in the shape of a loaf for ease of slicing. It has a supple texture, is dotted with small holes and is a rich shiny yellow in colour. During its ripening period large quantities of salt are added, which gives the cheese's surface a yellowish-white, lacquer-like coating. In taste, not overpowering, but sharpish, slightly sour.

Wines: Light whites and reds.
Serve: End of meals, snacks; the Germans recommend the cheese with sausage, ham and mushrooms.
Fat content: 45 per cent.
Type: Monastery.
Aroma: Unpronounced.

WINDSOR RED

Country of origin: Great Britain (England).

Background: In recent years several English companies have taken to making variations of traditional English cheeses. This is one—a blend of Cheddar with red wine.

Description: Windsor Red is an attractive-looking cheese, pale yellow in colour, mottled with red veining throughout; it looks good on a cheese board. The cheese is aged up to five months and has the characteristic clean, creamy Cheddar taste with a light flavour of red wine. Windsor Red is a close textured cheese, firm and slightly crumbly.

Wines: Light reds; beer.
Serve: End of meals; snacks.
Fat content: 45 per cent.
Type: Cheddar family.
Aroma: Unpronounced.

WORIENER

Another German cheese that is related to Limburger. The cheese is made in small 10 cm (4 in) square shapes.
(See *Limburger*.)

YOUNG AMERICAN

(See American *Cheddars*.)

ZIGER

A whey, Cottage style cheese, the best known version of which is Ricotta.
(See *Ricotta*.)

ZOMMA

A Turkish sheep's milk cheese similar to the better known Balkan cheese Kashkaval.
(See *Kashkaval*.)

Windsor Red (top), Derby Sage (below)

A

acid flavour 17
Allgau Emmentaler 21
Alpkäse 21
Altapol 20, 21
Altesse 21
Ambrosia 21, 22
American Edam 23
American Emmentaler 23
ammonia flavour 17
Anchor 23
Androuet, Pierre 12
Anejo 125
Anfrom 23
Angelot 120
annatto dye 18
à point 44
Appenzell 23
Appenzell Rass 23
Aristaeus 8
aroma 18
Asiago 23
Attiki Feta 73
Australian Edam 24
Australian Emmentaler 24
Australian Gouda 24
Australian Gruyère 24
Austrian Emmentaler 24, 69
Austrian Gruyère 24
Auvernois 123

B

Babybel 24
Baby Edam 25
Baby Gouda 25, 83
Backsteiner 25
Bacon Flavoured Cheddar 25
Bagozzo 25
Banon 25
Banon au Pèbre d'Ai 25, 119
Baraka 25
'barnyardy' aroma 18
Bauerhand 25
Bavarian 123
Bavarian Blue 26, 31, 33
Bayernland 26, 123
Beaufort 26
Beaumont 26
Beau Pasteur 27
Beer Cheese 27
Bega 27
Beguin 27
Bella Alpina 27
Bella Milano 27
Belle Bressane 27
Bellelaye 27
Bellétoile 27, 151
Bel Paese 27, 28

Bel Piano Lombardo 27
Bergkäse 29
Biarom 29
Bierkäse see Beer Cheese
Bitto 29
Bjelke Blue 29
Blå Castello 30
Black Diamond 29
Black Wax see Cheddar, American
bland cheeses 13
Bleu d'Auvergne 33
Bleu de Bresse 29, 33
Bleu de Gex 33
    see also Bleu du Haut Jura
Bleu des Causses 33
Bleu de Corse 30
Bleu du Haut Jura 30
Bleus 30
bloomy rind cheeses 18
Blue Castello 30, 31, 33
Blue Cheshire 33, 55
Blue Veins 13, 32, 33, 35
Blue Vinny 34
Bodalla see Cheddars, Australian
Bolina 32, 33
    see also Blue Veins
Bonbel 36
Bondon 36
Boulette d'Avesnes 36
Boulette de Cambrai 36
Boulette de la Pierre-Qui-Vire 37
Boursault 37
Boursin 37
Braided Cheese 37
    see also Spiced Cheese
Bresciano 37
Bressan 39
Bresse Bleu see Bleu de Bresse
Brick 38, 39
Brie 39, 40
Brie de Coulommiers see Coulommiers
Brie style cheeses 13
Brillat-Savarin 41
Brinza 42
Brioler 42
    see also Limburger
Briquette 42
    see also Neufchâtel
Brocotte 42
    see also Ricotta
Brod 42
    see also Elbo
brushed rind cheeses 18
Bucheron 42
    see also Chèvres
Buko 42
    see also Processed Cheese

Bulgarian Feta 72, 73
Burriello 42
Burrino 42
Burro 42
Butirro 42
Butter Cheese 43
buttery cheeses 13

C

Cabichou see Chabichou
Caboc 43
    see also Double Crèmes
Cabrion 43
    see also Chèvres
Caciocavallo 43
Cacio Fiore 44
Caciotta 44
    see also Stracchino
Caerphilly 44, 155
Calcagno 44
    see also Pecorino Romano
calorie content 7
Camembert 44, 45, 46
Camembert style cheeses 13
Canadian Cheddar 52
Canestrato 47
    see also Pecorino Romano
canned cheeses 16
Cantal 47
Caprice des Dieux 48
Capricette 48
    see also Chèvres
Caprino 48
Caprino Romano 48
    see also Pecorino Romano
Carré de l'Est 48
casein 18
Casigiolu 48
Cendrés 49
Chabi 49
Chabichou 49
'champion' cheeses 63
Chaource 49
Chaumes 49
    see also Limburger
Chavignol 49
    see also Crottin de Chavignol
Cheddar 49, 50
cheddaring 18
Cheddar style cheeses 13
Cheedam 52
cheesemaking 8
cheese types 12
Cherry Hill 52
    see also Cheddars, Canadian
Cheshire 54, 55
Chester 55
Chèvre du Montrachet 109
Chèvres 55

Chevrotin 55
Chevrotin de Conne 56
Chevrotin de Moulins 56
Chevrotin de Souvigny 56
Chilberta 56
close texture 18
Coeur 56
Coeur à la Crème 56
Colby 56
Coldpack Cheese 56
Colorado Blackie see Cheddars, American
Commissie 56
Comté 57
cooked cheeses 18
Coon 57
Cornhusker 57
Corolle du Poitou 57
Cotherstone 57
Cotswold 57
Cottage Cheese 57, 58
Coulommiers 59
Cream Cheese 59
Creamed Cottage Cheese 58, 59
Crema Dania 60
Creme Cherry 60, 123
Crème de Gruyère 60
    see also Processed Cheese
Crème de Savoie 60
    see also Processed Cheese
Crème Royale 60
    see also Crema Dania
Creole 61
Crescenza 61
Crottin de Chavignol 61
Cumin Cheddar 61
curdling process 11, 18
Curé Nantais 113
curing process 11, 18

D

Daisy see Cheddar, American
Damenkäse 61
    see also Butter Cheese
Danablu 32, 34, 61
Danbo 62
Danish Chef 62
Danish Edam 108
Danish Fontina 62
Danish Gorgonzola 113
Danish Saint Paulin 62
Danish Steppe 62
Dauphin 62
Délice de Saint-Cyr 62
Demi-Sel 62
Derby 63, 64
Derby Sage 63, 156
Dolcelatte 63
Domiati 63
Double Crèmes 12, 63

Double Gloucester *64*, 65
Doux de Montagne 65
Doux de Campagne 65
dry matter 18
Dry Ricotta 129
Duet 34, 66
Dunlop 66
Dutch Cheese *see* Cottage
  Cheese
Dutch Mature Gouda 83

E
Edam 66, *67*
Edelpilz 66
  see also German Blue
Ekte 68
Elbo 68
Emiliano 68
Emmentaler 68, *69*
Epicure 70
Epoisses 70
Erbo 70
  see also Blue Veins
Esrom 70, *71*
Excelsior 73
l'Explorateur 98
extra-hard cheeses 13
'eyes' in cheese 18

F
Fadiman, Clifton 123
Farm 73
Farmer Cheese 73
Farmhouse Cheddar *50, 51*
  see also Cheddar
fat content 7, 18
Fermier 73
Feta *72*, 73
Fin de Siècle 74
Finnish Emmentaler 74
'Five-Striper' *see* Livarot
flavoured cheeses 15
Fol Amour 74
Fontainebleau 74
Fontal 74
Fontina 74
Fontinella 75
Formaggini 75
Fourme d'Ambert 75
  see also Blue Veins
Fourme de Montbrison 75
Fourme de Pierre sur Haute
  75
freezing cheese 16
French Edam 75
French Gruyère 75
Fresco 75
fresh cheeses 12, 18
Friesian 75
Fromage à la Crème 76
Fromage à la Pie 73

Fromage Blanc 76
Fromage du Curé 113
Fromage Fondu 76
Fromage Fort 76
Fynbo 76, *149*

G
Gammelost 77
Gaperon 77
Gapron *see* Gaperon
Garlic Cheddar 78
Geheimratskäse 139
German Blue 78
  see also Blue Veins
German Edam 78
German Feta 72, *73*
German Gouda 78
German Port du Salut *see*
  Biarom
Gérômé 78
Gervais 78
Gex 33, 80
  see also Bleus
Gjetöst 79, 80
Glarenkäse 80
Glaren Schabziger 80
Glarnerkäse 80
goat's milk cheeses 13
  see also Chèvres
Gold'n Rich 80
Gorgonzola 80, *81*
  see also Blue Veins
Gouda *82*, 83
Gourmandise 83, *124*
Gournay 83
Gräddost 83
Grana 84
Grana Padano 84
Grand Vatel 84
Grappe 84
  see also La Grappe
Green Cheese 84
Grünland 84, *124*
Gruyère *85*, 86
Gruyère de Beaufort *see*
  Beaufort
Gruyère de Comté 86
  see also Comté

H
Haloumy 86
Hand 86
Harel, Madame Marie 44
Harz 87
Havarti 87, *88*
Herrgård Elite 89
Herrgårdsost 89
Hervé 89
Hick-o-ry 90
history 8
holes in cheese 18

Holyland 90

I
Ilchester 90
Incanestrato 90
inoculation process 11

J
Jalapeno 90
Jarlsberg 90, *91*
Jerome *92*, 93

K
Kameruka *see* Cheddar,
  Australian
Kanter 93
Kanter Kaas 93
Kareish 93
Kashkaval 93, *94*
Kasseri 93, *94*
Katschkawalj 93
Kaukauna Klub 95
keeping cheese 16
Kefalotyri *94*, 95
Kernhem 95
King Christian IX 95, *136*
Kleinkäse 95
Korb 95
Kosher cheese 90
Krauterkäse 95
Kuminost 95

L
La Bouille 96
La Grappe 96
Lamb, Charles 65
Lancashire 96, *97*
Lancashire Sage 96, *142*
Lapland 96
Larron 96
Laughing Cow 96
La Vache Qui Rit 96
Layton, T. E. 123
Leicester *97*, 98
l'Explorateur 98
Leyden 98, *99*
Liederkranz 98, *100*
Limburger 101
Liptauer 101
Livarot 101
Loaf 102
Lodigiano 102
Lombardo 102
Longhorn 102
Lucullus 102

M
Maconnais 102
MacRobertson *see* Cheddar,
  Australian
Magnum 102

Maigre 73
Mainland *see* Cheddar,
  New Zealand
Mainz 103
Malakoff 103
Manchego 103
Manteca 103
Manteche 42
Maori Gouda 103
Margotin 103
Maribo 104, *149*
Maroilles 104
Mascarpone 104, *105*
matière grasse 65
Mature Edam 106
Mature Gouda 83, 106
maturing process 11
Mejette 106
'meshanger' cheeses 95
Middebare 106
Milano 106
Milkana 106
Mimolette 106, *107*
Mini Esrom 106
Mini Fynbo 108, *149*
Mitzithra 108
Moe 108
Molbo 108, *149*
monastery cheeses 13
Moncenisio 108
Mon Chou 108
Monseer 108
Monsieur 109
Montasio 109
Monterey Jack 109
  see also Cheddar, American
Monthéry 109
Montrachet 109
Morbier 111
Mothais 111
  see also Chèvres
Mou 73
moulds 19
Mountain Boy 108
Mozzarella *15, 110*, 111
Mun-Chee 145
Münster 111
Mycella *32*, 113
  see also Blue Veins
Mynster *112*, 113
Mysöst 113

N
Nantais 113
Nebraska Agricultural
  Experiment Station 57
Nec Plus Extra *see* Processed
  Cheese
Netherlands Institute for
  Dairy Research 95
Neufchâtel 114

New Zealand Blue 34, 114
New Zealand Cheddar 52, 53
Nielson, Hanne 87
Nokkelöst 114
Norwegian Blue 35, 114
Norwegian Edam 115
Norwegian Emmentaler 115
Norwegian Saint Paulin 115

O
Oka 115
Okato Matured 115
 see also Cheddar, New Zealand
Olivet 115
Olivet Bleu 115
Olivet Cendré 115
Olmützer Quargel 115

P
Panedda 115
Pannerone 116
paraffin coating 19
Parmesan 116, 117
Parmigiano see Parmesan
Pasta Filata 116
pasteurisation 12
Pastorello 118
Pecorino Romano 118
Pecorino Sardo 118
Pecorino Siciliano 118
Penicillium candidum 13, 18, 19
P. glaucum 19
P. roqueforti 19
Pepato 118
Peperoni 119
Perfect Feta 74
Petit Suisse 119
Philadelphia 119
Pickled Cheese 119
Pineapple 119
 see also Cheddar, American
Pipo Crem' 119
Poivre d'Ane 119
Pont l'Evêque 120, 121
Poona 120
Popcorn Cheese see Cottage Cheese
Port Salut 120
Port Wine Cheddar 52, 53
Port Wine Stilton 144
Pot Cheese see Cottage Cheese
Pouligny-Saint-Pierre 123
Processed Cheese 15, 122, 123
protein content 7
Provoletti 124

Provolone 15, 124
Pyramide 125

Q
Quardo 125
Quargel 141
Quark 125
Quart 125
Queso Anejo 125
Queso Blanco 125
Queso Enchilado 125

R
Raclette 125
Ragnit 127
Rambol 124, 127
Rass see Appenzell Rass
Reblochon 127
Recuit 127
Red Cheshire 55, 126, 127
Redskin see Cheddar, American
Regal Picon 127
Remoudou 127
rennet 8, 19
Reybier 129
Ricotta 128, 129
Ricotta Salata 129
Ridder 129
rindless cheeses 16
rinds 11, 19
ripening process 11
Riviana 131
Robiola 131
Rollot 131
Romadur 131
Romano 131
Rondelé 131, 151
Roquefort 130, 131
Roschmier 132
Royalp 132, 133

S
Saanen 132
Saga 132
Sage 134
Saint André 134
Saint Benoit 134
Saint Marcellin 134
Saint Maure 134
Saint Nectaire 134
Saint Otho 137
Saint Paulin 135, 137
Saisof 41
salting process 11
Samos 90 124, 137
Samsoe 136, 137, 149
Sapsago 138
Sardo 138
Savoia 27
Sbrinz 133, 138

Scarmorza 138
Schabzier 139
Schmierkäse see Cottage Cheese
Schnittkäse 139
Schottenziger 139
Schweizer 139
Selles-sur-Cher 139
Septmoncel 139
Serac 139
Serra da Estrella 139
sheep's milk cheeses 15
Simon, Andre 123
Single Gloucester 65
skimmed milk 19
Slipcote 141
Smoked Cheese 15, 140, 141
Sorbais 141
Sour Curd Cheese 141
Southbrook Cheshire 54, 142
Spalen 142
Spiced Cheeses 15, 142
Spiced Gouda 142
 see also Gouda
Spitz 142
Stangen 142
starters 8, 11, 19
Steinbüscher 142
Stilton 143, 144
storing cheese 16
Stracchino 144
Stracchino di Milano 106
Stracchino Dolce 144
Stracchino Piccante 144
strong-smelling cheeses 15
Suprême des Ducs 145
Sveciaost 145
Swedish Fontina 145
Sweet Muenster 145
Sweitzer see Schweizer
Swiss style cheeses 13

T
Taffel 145
Taleggio 146
Telemes 146
Tête de Moine 146
Texas Longhorn see Longhorn
texture 19
Tholstrup, Henrik 60
Thurgauer 146
Tiger 124, 146
Tillamook 148
Tilsit 147, 148
Tomme au Fenouil 148
Tomme au Marc 148
Tomme Boudane 148
Tomme de Chèvres 148
Tomme de Savoie 148

Tommes 148
Tommes des Neiges 148
Tommes des Pyrenees 148
Tomme du Poitou 148
Tomme du Revard 148
Trappist 150
Treccia 150
Triple Crèmes 12, 150, 151
Tropefynbo 152
Twin Flats see Cheddar, American
Tybo 149, 152

U
Unity Blue 35, 152
unripened cheeses 12

V
Vacchino Romano 152
Vache Qui Rit 96
Vacherin d'Abondance 153
Vacherin des Aillons 153
Vacherin des Beauges 153
Vacherin Fribourgeois 152
Vacherin Mont d'Or 153
Valais Raclette 153
 see also Raclette
Valembert 153
Valençay 153
Veneto 153
Venezza 153
Vermont 52, 154
Vermont Sage 52, 134, 154
Vieux Pané 154
'Vieux Puant' 104
Vittoria 27

W
Warsawski 154
washed rind cheeses 19
wax coating 19
Weisslacker 154
Wensleydale 154, 155
whey cheeses 15
White Cheshire 55
White Gorgonzola 157
White Stilton 157
Wilstermarsch 157
Windsor Red 156, 157
wine and cheese 16
Woriener 157

Y
Yorkshire Stilton see Cotherstone
Young American see Cheddar, American

Z
Ziger 157
Zomma 157